# HAUSA FOLKTALES FROM NIGER

# HAUSA FOLKTALES FROM NIGER

Translated and Edited

by

**Robert S. Glew and Chaibou Babalé**

Ohio University Center for International Studies
Monographs in International Studies

Africa Series Number 63
Athens, Ohio 1993

**Library of Congress Cataloging-in-Publication Data**

Hausa folktales from Niger / translated and edited by Robert
S. Glew and Chaibou Babalé.
    p.   cm. – ( Monographs in international studies.
Africa series; no. 63)
      ISBN 0-89680-176-4
      1. Hausa (African people) –Folklore.   I. Glew,
Robert S.  II. Babalé, Chaibou.  III. Series.
GR351.92.H38H38   1993
398.2'096626–dc20            92-41991
                                CIP

99 98 97 96 95 94 93       5 4 3 2 1

# CONTENTS

# PREFACE

The folktales in this collection were first broadcast, in Hausa, between October, 1989 and September, 1990 on Niger's national radio station. During the first of two years I worked in Niger as a U.S. Peace Corps Volunteer I recorded these tales and asked my good friend Chaibou Babalé to undertake the painstaking task of transcribing them. The following year was spent translating the tales into English. It is hoped that people interested in African folklore will find this collection of folktales useful and enjoyable.

I wish to express my thanks to the people who have taught me Hausa, without whose instruction this work would not have been possible. Specifically, Linda Hunter and Neil Skinner from the University of Wisconsin at Madison; John Hutchinson and Jennifer Yanco from Boston University; Hassana and Ousseina Alidou from the University of Niamey; and Yazi Dogo and Abdou Lushé from l'Institut National de Documentation de Recherche et d'Animation Pédagogiques, Niamey. I also wish to acknowledge Harold Scheub and Daniel Kunene from the University of Wisconsin at Madison for stimulating my interest in African oral tradition. And finally, thank you to Margo Glew who spent many hours entering the translations on the computer and proofreading the work.

# INTRODUCTION

The folklore of Hausa storytellers Hadjia Rahamu and Hadjia Angèle has been heard on Niger's national radio station for over eighteen years. These performers' popularity is evident throughout Niger as their familiar voices are listened to by children and adults alike with equal enthusiasm. They tell tales of Gizo, the spider-trickster; Hyena, the greedy buffoon; Snake and many other animals. Other tales operate in the realm of man, many dealing with a boy or a girl who is undergoing a process of maturation.

The storytellers employ reality and fantasy as they draw from a countless number of motifs and images in the telling of their tales. In addition to entertaining people, the tales often reflect the values and expected behavior of society. According to both storytellers the importance of these tales lies in their value as an educational tool for children. They deal with the importance of respecting one's elders, the undesirability of greed and the importance of trust. The consequences of disregarding these values are clear as disrespect, greed and betrayal are usually met with harsh consequences. Hadjia Rahamu is proud to serve in this role and she is pleased when children express interest in the tales. She is especially happy when children come to her with their questions about life.

Hadjia Rahamu was born and raised in Zinder, a city about 600 miles east of Niamey, Niger's capital. She learned to perform tales from her mother, who often told the children tales to keep them in their compounds at night. By watching and listening to her mother's performances, and then practicing them with other children, Hadjia Rahamu became an adept storyteller. Now she is passing this skill on to her grandchildren by performing the tales for them. Not all of them are interested, however, and unlike the children of her youth, some prefer to go into town and socialize with their friends.

Hadjia Angèle was also born and raised in Zinder. Like Hadjia Rahamu, she learned to perform tales during her childhood. In the evening she would gather with her friends and tell tales. Often times old women would tell tales to them. She recalls one woman in particular who would invite children to her compound when her husband went out of town. She allowed the children to sleep at her home and told them tales late into the night. Hadjia Angèle remembers these tales and performs them today. She encourages her children and grandchildren to perform the tales, but like Hadjia Rahamu, she agrees that today's children are unlike those of former times. She remarks that while some children record her performances on cassette tape and write them in notebooks, others have little interest in the tradition.

When Hadjia Rahamu and Hadjia Angèle began performing on the radio they selected the tales they told. Shortly thereafter their grandchildren began requesting certain tales and other people from Zinder followed with their requests. Now they receive children's letters from all over Niger, and even Nigeria, asking for performances of their favorite tales. Hadjia Rahamu and Hadjia Angèle choose the most requested tales for their weekly, thirty minute radio program. The storyteller who is most familiar with the request performs the tale or tales for that week. The performances are recorded in the local radio and television studio in Zinder and sent to Niamey where they are broadcast nationally the following week.

Both storytellers enjoy performing on the radio and hope to continue their work there. If the many people gathered around their radios and listening to the broadcasts have any say they will be performing for a long time to come.

# TALES TOLD

## BY

## HADJIA ANGÈLE

## THE TOMCAT AND THE CHICKEN

This tale is about Chicken and Rooster who lived together. One day a large tomcat heard about them. Whenever Chicken laid eggs Tomcat came and ate them. No matter where she hatched her children Tomcat came and ate them. This caused Chicken to worry, and her chest feathers became worn down from hatching so many eggs.

Her strength was almost gone when she told her husband, "We have to move to a place that will be safe for our eggs and children. Tomcat has been eating our children and won't stop until he has eaten all of us. We must pack our belongings and leave this place." "Okay, I agree," he said, and they moved.

Tomcat went to their house, but there was no one there. He stood where he had previously been able to find food in abundance. He wondered, "Did someone kill them or did they move?"

Meanwhile Chicken and Rooster found a new place to live where God gave them a beautiful family. They lived happily with their children and even their grandchildren.

Tomcat searched everywhere for them until he discovered where they were living. He said, "Ah! They've moved! What should I bring with me when I go to visit them? Now there are many of them. I must be careful because if I go to their house and they recognize me they'll kill me." Then he said, "Wait, I've thought of something. I'll take a drum to play music for them. If God wills it I'll catch them." And Tomcat made a drum.

Chicken and Rooster thought they were safe. Then one day Tomcat went to Chicken's house and greeted them. They greeted Tomcat, gave him some food and invited him into their house. Chicken said, "Husband?" "Yes," he replied. "Is this the tomcat who used to come and eat our family?" "Well, he looks like him, but the other tomcat didn't have a drum. He wasn't a drummer, but this tomcat does resemble him," he said.

3

Tomcat told Chicken, "This afternoon I'll play my drum." "Well this house is full of children, and they'll be happy to listen to you," she said.

That afternoon Tomcat began playing and sang, "Cock-a-doodle-doo, in this world it's chicken who says cock-a-doodle-doo!" Chicken danced, wildly beating her wings, and said, "My excellent drummer who is playing for me, take one of my children as a reward for your drumming." Tomcat took a child away and ate it.

The next day Tomcat returned to the house and again played for Chicken. When he finished she gave him another child, and he carried it away and ate it.

Rooster asked his wife, "Do you realize that since this drummer has been coming here we've been losing our children? Is this the same tomcat as before?" "No, it's not him," Chicken replied. This continued until all of their children had been eaten and only Chicken and Rooster remained. The drummer did not visit them for a while.

One day he returned and sang, "Cock-a-doodle-doo, in this world it's Chicken who says cock-a-doodle-doo!" Chicken said, "My excellent drummer who is playing for me, take my husband as a reward for your drumming." Tomcat took Rooster away and ate him. Rooster screamed and screamed as Tomcat carried him away. Now only Chicken remained.

A week passed and Tomcat returned. She wondered, "Does he want to eat me, or does he want something else?" Tomcat sang, "Cock-a-doodle-doo, in this world it's Chicken who says cock-a-doodle-doo!" When he finished Chicken said, "My excellent drummer, drummer Tomcat, take my life as a reward for your drumming." Tomcat took Chicken away and ate her. At this time she knew it was Tomcat because she said, "My excellent drummer, drummer Tomcat." This is why tomcats like to eat chickens and why they follow them to their houses to catch them.

# THE HARE AND THE HYENA

One day the animals of the bush were hungry and did not know what to do. While Hare was travelling deep in the bush he saw a palm tree full of fruit. He threw something into the tree, and a piece of fruit fell to the ground. He went home and ate the fruit with his family. Whenever he went to this tree he picked a piece of fruit and brought it home to eat with his family.

One day he went to the tree, and there was only one piece of fruit left. He threw his stick at the fruit, and it fell from the tree into a hole. Hare was worried that his family would have nothing to eat, so he followed the fruit into the hole. The fruit rolled into a house and Hare continued to follow it. Hare met people in this house and worked for them. In return they gave him food to eat. When the people gave Hare work to do he never refused to do it or complained about it. When he realized he had been working there for a week he said, "Tomorrow I'm going home." And they said, "Okay."

In the morning a boy came and told Hare, "If you're told to go into a room and choose a stick be sure not to choose a large or beautiful stick. You must take a small stick which isn't very nice." When Hare went into the room he remembered the advice that the boy had given him and chose a small unattractive stick. The people told him to blow on the end of his stick when he returned to the bush.

After Hare travelled in the bush for some time he blew on the end of his stick. Millet, guinea corn, corn, rice and other grains poured out from the end of his stick. Hare told the town crier to call the townspeople and invite them to come and take some food. The people were pleased and came and took as much as they could carry. Everyone filled their granaries.

One day Hyena asked Hare where he found the stick which produced so much food when blown. Hare told Hyena, "I found it with the help of God." Hare did not want to tell her exactly where he got it. Every time Hyena came and asked Hare where he found the stick, he refused to tell her. Hare continued to invite people to come and take food.

One day Hyena came to Hare pretending to cry. Then she began flattering him to learn the secret. Hare finally asked her, "Do you want to know where I found the stick? I'm afraid to tell you because you always cause problems." Hyena said that she would be well behaved. Hare said, "Okay, I'll tell you, but if you go there and you're given work to do don't be argumentative." Hyena agreed so Hare said, "Then I'll tell you. Do you know the place deep in the bush where I used to pick fruit? You must go there. Take your stick and throw it into the tree. When a fruit falls into a hole you must follow it. It will go into a house, and it's in this house that you'll be given a stick. Remember, no matter how much work they give you don't be argumentative." Hyena said, "Okay."

Hyena took a stick and travelled deep into the bush to the tree where Hare picked fruit. She threw her stick into the tree, and a piece of fruit fell to the ground and into the hole. She followed it into the hole and then into the house. Hyena, however, refused to do any of the work given to her.

Because she was greedy and impatient, Hyena announced that she was going home after only two days. In the morning the boy came and said, "If someone tells you to go into this room and take a stick don't choose a large or beautiful stick. Take a small stick which is not very nice." Hyena agreed, went into the room and chose a large, beautiful stick and prepared to leave.

The people told her, "When you return to the bush blow on the stick to produce food." When Hyena returned home she told the town crier to call all of the townspeople to come and take some food. Hare said, "For God's sake, don't go. Don't you know that Hyena is always causing problems?" Some people listened to Hare, and others said he was jealous. Hyena blew on one end of the stick, and scorpions, snakes, biting ants and wild animals of the bush came out and attacked the people. Everyone ran as fast as they could.

## THE DOG AND THE HYENA

This tale is about Dog, Rooster, and Hyena. Dog and Rooster were friends. One day they took a sack and went to a naming ceremony. They had been travelling for a long time when they saw Cat in the distance. Rooster told Dog, "Hey, Cat's coming! Let me hide in the sack. If Cat asks you what you're carrying tell him guinea corn." Dog said, "Okay."

When Cat arrived he asked, "Mister Dog, what are you carrying?" "Only some guinea corn," Dog answered. "I'm on my way to a naming ceremony." Cat said, "You may continue."

When Cat was far away, Dog saw Hyena in the distance and said, "Rooster, Rooster! Come out quickly, I must hide in the sack!" Rooster carried the sack over his shoulder. He travelled a short distance and came face to face with Hyena who asked, "What are you carrying Rooster?" Rooster said, "Only some guinea corn. I'm going to a naming ceremony."

After Hyena started to walk away, Rooster said, "Look Hyena, actually I'm carrying Dog!" Hyena quickly returned, caught Dog, tied him up and took him to her house. She told her children, "Guard him well. I'm going to collect some wood so we can cook him."

Dog took out some charcoal and began eating it. When Hyena's daughter saw him she asked, "Hey, what are you eating?" "Charcoal," Dog told her. Hyena's daughter said, "Give me a little." Dog refused and she begged and begged.

After some time Dog said, "I'll give you some, but only after you've given me a toy to play with and the clothes you're wearing." She continued to beg.

More time passed and Dog again told her, "I'll give you some, but only after you've given me a toy to play with and the clothes you're wearing. Also, you must come and sit here so I can tie you up." Finally she agreed, and he gave her some charcoal and tied her up. She began eating the charcoal.

When Hyena returned she asked, "Where's Dog?" Pretending to be her daughter Dog said, "He's over there." Then he ran away. Hyena boiled some water and began cooking her daughter thinking that it was Dog. After some time Dog returned and said, "It was your own daughter that you put in the water!" Then he ran away again. Hyena took her daughter out of the water and saw that she was severely burned. She chased Dog, cornered him in a hole and caught him. She told her son to guard Dog and then went to look for some wood to build a fire.

Dog told Hyena's son, "I can run very fast. If you let me go I'll show you how fast I can run from here to there." Hyena's son released Dog who ran a short distance after which Hyena's children followed him and caught him. They said, "You're right puppy, you really run fast." Dog told them, "If you release me again I'll run to that small hill over there." They released him and Dog ran to the small hill where he met Hyena. She tried to catch him, but he dodged her. She threw sand at him and said, "Bastard! I have a dog who's better than you tied up at my house."

When she arrived home she asked, "Where's the puppy?" Her children said, "He runs very fast. We set him free and he showed us his speed." Hyena said, "So it was him I met. You little bastards! Now I'm going to kill you!"

# THE DONKEY WHO PRETENDED TO HAVE HORNS

There is an expression in Hausa which says: "If a donkey had horns in place of his ears he would be a malicious animal." That is how it is.

One day Donkey heard this with his own ears and went to the watering hole where Lion, Elephant and all the other animals came to drink. At this time Donkey lived in the bush with the rest of the animals. The animals were afraid of Donkey because of his voice. Lion became his friend, and together they terrorized the other animals.

One morning, when none of the animals had drunk any water and were very thirsty, they all got together and held a meeting. Elephant led the way to the meeting. Suddenly Donkey began screaming, "Hee-haw, hee-haw, hee-haw!" All of the animals were afraid. In the panic the animals who were able to run ran away. Elephant trampled some of the other animals. Antelope and Camel also ran. Lion brought home Giraffe's trampled corpse and ate it for two days. The delicious meat lasted for two weeks.

Lion encouraged his friend Donkey to be even more malicious. Donkey went back to the watering hole so that none of the animals could drink. All of the animals were thirsty, but did not know what to do and were afraid. Thirst gripped them like never before. None of the animals dared go near the watering hole because they were afraid of Donkey. They were afraid that Donkey would catch them and kill them. Everyone tried to think of a solution because they were dying of thirst.

Then Hare, the cleverest of all animals of the bush, told them that he wanted to meet with them to discuss the problem. He suggested that they go and respectfully talk to Snake about their problem. The animals agreed to go and see Snake and set out for his house.

Along the way they came to Donkey's house, and Hare stopped them. He went forward to the watering hole. As usual Donkey

9

began to cry, "Hee-haw, hee-haw, hee-haw," while he farted powerfully. Hare cried out, "Don't be afraid! It's only Donkey scaring us. Those aren't horns which can stab us, they're his ears!" "You're lying!" the animals said. "Donkey has sharp horns!" "Wait, you'll see," said Hare. Donkey came up to Hare and lowered his head as if to stab him. Hare grabbed Donkey's ears and called the other animals to help him. "You see, these are ears, not horns! Come and beat him!" All of the animals beat Donkey, tied him to a tree with a rope and returned to the bush.

After some time a man passed by with a bundle of wood and found Donkey tied to the tree. He untied him, loaded him with his wood and went to town. This is the reason that donkeys are found in town.

# THE GUINEA FOWL, THE JACKAL, AND THE VULTURE

One day Guinea Fowl was sitting in a tree. Jackal came and sat in the shade under the tree where she was laying eggs and said, "Arutu-tu-tu-tu," and she gave him an egg, and he ate it. Time passed and Guinea Fowl laid many eggs. But because she kept giving them to Jackal she never had any children.

One day Vulture was flying overhead when she saw Guinea Fowl from a distance. She landed and asked, "Guinea Fowl, I've seen you lay many eggs. Where are all of your children?" Guinea Fowl replied, "Jackal comes and says, 'Arutu-tu-tu-tu,' and I give him an egg, and he eats it." "Stop giving him eggs," Vulture said. "The next time he comes tell him to climb the tree and get an egg himself." Guinea Fowl agreed.

After some time Jackal came and said, "Arutu-tu-tu-tu." "Today you must climb the tree by yourself to get an egg," Guinea Fowl told him. Jackal tried to climb the tree but fell down. Blaming the fall on his sandals, he took them off and tried to climb the tree again. But he slipped and fell again. This time he said it was because of his hat, so he took it off and put it aside.

Jackal had spent a long time tricking Guinea Fowl out of her eggs and eating them. But Vulture taught Guinea Fowl some trickery to prevent him from taking her eggs. Jackal, however, always has to get the best of everyone, so he wanted to know how Guinea Fowl learned this trick. Jackal, who was very angry now, asked everyone what had come between him and Guinea Fowl.

Finally, Jackal went to Guinea Fowl and said, "Guinea Fowl?" "Yes?" she replied. "Who taught you this cleverness?" Guinea Fowl said, "Do you think I'm going to tell you it was Vulture? I refuse, I'm not going to tell you it was Vulture." Jackal left and thought, "So that's who it was. Now I understand."

Jackal went to the garbage heap and laid down with his mouth open pretending to be dead. After some time Vulture passed by and saw him. Thinking he was dead she landed on his mouth and pushed on it several times to be sure he was not alive. Then Jackal quickly grabbed Vulture who said, "Today I've encountered an evil thing." Jackal told Vulture, "Either carry me to the market in the sky or be eaten. It's your choice." Vulture replied, "Wait, I'll carry you to the market in the sky. But if I carry you and we pass the small market and someone shouts, 'There's Jackal and Vulture,' be silent. If we pass the large market and someone shouts, 'There's Jackal and Vulture,' tell them it's none of their business." Jackal agreed and they took off.

When they came to the small market someone shouted, "Look, Jackal and Vulture!" and Jackal was silent. Then they came to the large market and someone shouted, "Look, Jackal and Vulture!" Jackal said, "It's none of your. . . ." As he was speaking, Jackal fell into the area where the butchers were butchering some animals. They grabbed him, tied him up and beat him. That is the reason you do not find Jackal, Vulture and Guinea Fowl in the same place.

## THE MAN AND THE CROCODILE

Once there was a man who travelled into the bush to collect tall grass with which he did his weaving. He could do anything with straw. Nearby there was an old crocodile who lived in a river. Hunters had been unsuccessfully trying to catch this crocodile for a long time.

One day Crocodile asked for trouble by leaving the river and climbing a hill. By coincidence the hunters had gathered in a large group that day. Crocodile climbed the hill and then heard the beat of the hunters' drum. As Crocodile listened to the drum one of the hunters, who had excellent eyesight, saw him.

The hunter said, "Until now we've been unable to catch Crocodile. Today we'll catch him no matter where he goes," and they began running after him. The men chased Crocodile and he ran. But, by the grace of God, the men were unable to catch him.

Along the road Crocodile noticed the man collecting straw and stopped. When the man saw him coming he said, "My God!" and began to run. Crocodile called after the man, "Please, for God's sake don't run away. Please stop and help me." The man stopped and asked, "What can I do for you?" Crocodile said, "Do you see that cloud of dust coming? Hunters are following me and trying to catch me. Today I tried to do something I shouldn't have done. I tried to climb a hill. As you know crocodiles aren't good at climbing hills because we're not at home out of the water. Please hide me in your straw, I who still have grandchildren in the water." The man asked, "How in the name of God am I going to hide you?" Crocodile told him, "Hide me in the straw. It'll hold me, you know that." The man asked, "How can a crocodile be hidden in straw?" Crocodile said, "Unroll the straw." The man unrolled his bundle of straw and Crocodile laid on top of it. Crocodile said, "Take some straw from over there and cover me with it." After the man covered him Crocodile said, "Now take the ends, tie them up and stand the

13

bundle upright. After you've put the bundle on end no one will know that there's a crocodile inside."

The man did everything Crocodile asked him to do. After some time the hunters arrived shouting, "Hey you! Hey you!" When the man saw them he acted surprised and said, "What is it?" "We're chasing Crocodile. We're following his tracks and they end here," they said. "What?" the man asked. "Crocodile!" they shouted.

The man said, "In the name of God! Look at how many of you there are chasing him. I'm here all by myself. Would I still be here if Crocodile came by? Anyway, how could something hide in this heavy bundle of straw? Why would I be here hiding Crocodile when there are thirty of you chasing him? Stop bothering me, I haven't seen Crocodile. Do you think I put him in my pocket or swallowed him? Do you see any blood indicating that I slaughtered him?" They looked around for Crocodile but did not find him and left.

The man laid the roll of straw on its side, untied it and said, "Okay Crocodile, come out." Crocodile said, "Thank you, thank you, thank you. Will you please do one more thing for me?" The man asked, "Okay Crocodile what can I do for you?" "Because you were so kind to me I'll one day return the favor, so I want you to come and see where I live." The man said, "Wait a minute Crocodile. Everyone knows that crocodiles live in the river with the hippopotamuses and fish." Crocodile told him, "No, that's not how it is. Look at me. Among crocodiles I'm the largest. I'm a great crocodile!" "For God's sake Crocodile go away and leave me in my poverty," the man said. Crocodile persisted, "Hey, we're trusting friends, let's go. I want you to come and meet my large family."

Finally the man agreed. Crocodile led the way and the man followed. When they reached the river the man asked, "Is this where you come from?" "Yes," Crocodile said. "I see," said the man. "You don't understand," Crocodile said. "You must go into the water to see my home and meet my family because one day I'll return the favor you did for me." The man said, "Crocodile, I've seen the river. Now go to your home and I'll go to mine." Crocodile continued, "Come on! There's trust between friends. In the name of God we have trust between us!" "Because you said, 'in the name of God,' I agree," the man told him.

Crocodile entered the water, and the man began to follow him. He was impatient and could not wait for the man to be totally in the water. While the man had one foot in the water and one foot still on land, Crocodile grabbed the man's foot. The man asked, "Crocodile, why have you grabbed my foot?" He replied, "You know that men prevent me from coming on land to get what I want to eat. Now that I've caught you, you'll be my meat." "No, I won't be your meat," the man replied. "If God wills it, the trust I had in you will free me." Crocodile said, "You won't be free until I've eaten you." The two argued about trust and friendship.

They argued and argued until along came Jackal who had come to drink some water. When he saw the situation he said, "Hey you! How can a man fight with himself?" The man replied, "I'm caught. Crocodile is holding me." Jackal asked, "Crocodile? That's your problem!" He took off running and said, "This isn't a good place to drink water."

A short time later Jackal returned and asked the man, "Are you telling the truth? Does Crocodile really have a hold of you, or is this merely horseplay by the river?" Then Crocodile said, "Eee!" while still holding the man's foot. Jackal said, "Raise your head so that I can see you." Crocodile raised his head and said, "Here I am." Jackal asked, "What's the problem here? I can't mediate this dispute with one of you above water and the other below water. If you want me to help, you both must come on land. Neither of you can hold the other. Crocodile, release the man."

The man came out and Jackal said, "Crocodile, come out of the water if you want me to mediate this dispute." When Crocodile came on land Jackal asked, "What happened?" The man went and brought his bundle of straw. Jackal asked, "When this man unrolled the straw what did you do Crocodile?" "I laid down on it," he said. "Then what did you do?" Jackal asked the man. "I covered him with some straw like this." "After you covered him with straw did you leave him?" "No," the man said. "I rolled up the bundle and tied it." "Get some rope and tie it," said Jackal. The man took some rope and tied the bundle of straw three times. The man told Jackal, "You see, this is how I did it." "After you tied it what did you do?" asked Jackal. "I stood it on end," the man said. Jackal asked, "Do you eat crocodile meat at your house?" "Yes we do!" said the man. "What are you waiting for? Take the meat," Jackal told him. The man took Crocodile, who was inside his roll of straw, and left. For that reason if someone betrays your trust do not say anything to him. Be patient and God will help you.

## THE MALAM AND THE JACKAL

One day Jackal was wandering around in the bush. Having nothing better to do he said to himself, "I think I'll go into town and get some more cleverness." So he went and visited the most renowned malam in the town.

The malam asked, "Jackal, why are you so unhappy?" Jackal said, "My cleverness is not as strong as it once was, so I've come to you to learn to be more clever." The malam asked, "Jackal, don't you have anything better to do than come here and learn to be more clever?" "No, I don't. I've noticed that my cleverness is decreasing," Jackal told him.

The malam said, "I can teach you to be more clever, but in order for me to do so you must bring me five things. After you've done that everything you ask for will be given to you." "Okay, tell me the things that you need," Jackal said. "First, you must bring me a live puff-adder." Jackal asked, "How can I bring you a live puff-adder?" The malam replied, "You're clever enough to do that." "I've heard the first thing," Jackal said. The malam continued, "The second thing is some milk from a bush cow. The third, sleepy sand from a lion's eye, and the fourth, tears from an old woman." Jackal asked, "An old woman's tears?" "Yes," the malam said. "And the fifth thing you must show me is two elephants wrestling. If you bring me these things I'll give you all the cleverness you want by asking God to fulfill your needs." Jackal said, "Okay, but before I leave may I please have a basket?" The malam gave him a basket and he left.

Jackal went and found a puff-adder. He peeked into her hole, and pretending to speak to a monkey said, "You see you cowardly fool! You saw her and climbed a tree. I'm sure that she can fill this basket." "No she can't." Puff-Adder looked at Jackal and asked, "Who are you talking to?" Jackal said, "It's me and this stupid monkey. He said that if you get into this old basket you won't fill it. I said that you would fill it." "Where is he?" asked Puff-Adder.

Jackal said, "There he is, there in the tree looking at you." Puff-Adder told him, "Give me the basket and you'll see. I'll settle this dispute." He opened the basket and Puff-Adder crawled inside. Jackal closed the basket and tied it shut. Puff-Adder pleaded, "Jackal, please let me out, it's hot in here." Jackal asked, "Why would I let you out when I want to keep you there?"

He brought her to the malam who asked, "Is this it?" He looked inside and said, "Okay Jackal, that's the first thing." Then Jackal said, "May I please have a tree trunk with a hole in it to take with me?" The malam gave Jackal what he asked for, and Jackal left.

After some time he saw a bush cow. Jackal said, "Of course she can go into this hole. I went in and out, surely she can do it better than I did." "You're lying!" Bush Cow turned, looked at Jackal and said, "Jackal, who are you with?" Jackal said, "Oh, this stupid monkey said that even if you get a running start you can't enter the hole in this tree trunk." Bush Cow said, "Jackal, you who are smaller than I can do it better than I."

Jackal said, "Watch this," and ran toward the tree trunk in a cloud of dust. When he reached the tree trunk he returned to where he had started from. Bush Cow asked, "Where are you?" Jackal said, "Didn't you see what was in front of you? I went into the hole and came out." "If you went in and came out I can certainly do it because you're smaller and weaker than I," Bush Cow told him. She went back, charged the tree and got her head stuck in the hole. She pulled and pulled but could not get free.

She cried, "Hey Jackal, get me out!" "How can I get you out?" Jackal asked. "We've been here since this morning and I haven't had anything to eat or drink. I'm very hungry. I'll go and look for some food to eat and then I'll get you out." Bush Cow said, "There's milk here. After you drink some of my milk you can help me get free." Jackal agreed. He drank some milk and put some aside. When he had taken what he wanted he said, "If I'm the one who caused you to get stuck you're not getting free," and he left her there.

He brought the milk to the malam who asked, "Is this it?" "Yes it is," said Jackal. "Okay, that's the second thing." Jackal asked, "For the third thing may I have a small calabash bowl?", and the malam gave him one.

Jackal went into a house but did not see any old women. Then he remembered that there was a certain place where the king housed old women who did not have anyone to care for them. When he entered the house he said, "What's going on here? The king has gathered all the old women. They're crying and he's collecting their tears to be taken to Paradise." All the old women began crying.

Jackal collected the tears, went to the malam and said, "Here it is! Now I need some sweet millet balls. Do you know the type I want sir?" "I know," said the malam. "Please give me some," Jackal said. The millet balls were prepared and given to him.

Jackal went into the bush and began tasting the sweet millet balls. In the distance he saw Lion and hid. Lion came and said, "You bastard, what did you see that made you hide and cry?" Jackal said, "Oh, these tears are nothing father Lion." Lion asked, "Are you eating something?" Jackal said, "Father Lion, this small thing that I'm eating is for children. If I give you some you'll want me to get you some more and the place I got it from is far away. What I'm eating was given to me." Lion said, "Jackal, do you believe that just because you give me a little taste I'm going to catch you and force you to get me some more?" Jackal took a small bit of a sweet millet ball and gave it to Lion. Lion put it in his mouth and tasted how sweet it was. "Give me some more!" Lion shouted. Jackal gave him more and more until it was all gone. Lion grabbed Jackal and said, "I don't care where you have to go to get it, but you have to bring me some more." They argued about this for some time.

There were some monkeys in the tree above them who were laughing. Jackal raised his head and said, "There it is! I used monkey feces to make it." Lion told the largest monkey to come down. When the monkey came down Lion grabbed him and squeezed him until feces came out. Lion tasted the feces, but it tasted foul so he threw it aside. Jackal explained, "Father Lion, you didn't squeeze him hard enough. It's there deep inside of him."

While monkey was not looking Jackal put a little of the sweet millet ball around his anus so that Lion would taste it. Jackal told Lion, "If you put some sleepy sand from your eyes on his anus he'll defecate the same thing that I gave you and that you liked." Lion agreed, so Jackal took some sleepy sand out of Lion's eyes and put it on the monkey's anus. He kept the leftover sleepy sand and told Lion, "I'm going to go down the hill before monkey defecates."

Jackal escaped and left Lion and the monkey. He brought the sleepy sand to the malam and said, "Here's some sleepy sand from a lion's eyes." The malam said, "Okay, there's only one thing left." "What's that?" asked Jackal. "You must show me two elephants wrestling." "Very well," said Jackal. "But I need someone to make me a very thick rope. The kind that is used to tie a cow." The rope was made and given to Jackal.

Jackal walked through the bush until he met an elephant grazing. He began crying and Elephant asked, "What is it?" "My father has given me a difficult task," Jackal told her. "He has given me this rope and told me to stretch it. Oh, this is difficult work. How can I stretch this long rope by myself! What am I going to do?" Elephant said, "Let me have one end. Take the other end and find a large rock to tie it to. But don't tie it to a tree because when I pull I'll uproot it."

Jackal took the other end of the rope and travelled until he saw another elephant in the distance. He told her the same story and gave her the other end of the rope. Then he said, "I'm going to tie this end to a tree. I'll shout to you when it's time to pull." The malam was watching from a tree. Jackal shouted to the elephants and they began to pull each other. Then he returned to the tree where the malam was sitting. One elephant pulled, then the other elephant pulled. They wrestled like this for some time.

After a while the first elephant asked, "What's going on here? Let me follow this rope and see what's happening." The other elephant did the same. They both followed the rope and met in the middle. One elephant asked, "Who gave you this rope? How did you get it?" She said, "Jackal gave it to me." The other said, "He gave it to me also." She said, "Because he has made us wrestle, the next time we see him we'll kill him!" And they both let go of the rope.

Jackal asked the malam, "Did you see them wrestling? Let's go home so you can teach me to be more clever." The malam said, "There's one more thing." "What is it?" asked Jackal. "Go and bring me a large calabash bowl." "Where am I going to find that?" "Use your cleverness," the malam told him. Jackal brought the calabash bowl, and the malam said, "Okay, now let's go into the bush." When they reached the bush the malam asked, "Do you see that field over there?" "Yes," said Jackal. "Go over there and put the calabash bowl over you.  Underneath the bowl I'll teach you cleverness."

Jackal took the calabash bowl to the field, turned it upside down and hid nearby.  The malam ran up to the calabash bowl and smashed it to pieces.  He thought that Jackal was dead, but he appeared and said, "Malam, I'm not dead."  The malam said, "God saved you.  But if your cleverness is increased you'll be a nuisance to people."  Jackal said, "Now I can't go back into the bush because all of the animals are angry with me.  I've caused problems everywhere.  What can I do now?"

Jackal went into the bush where he came across a dead antelope.  He took the antelope's skin and put it on.  Jackal looked like an antelope.  He outsmarted them all, but the other animals would not talk to him.

# GIZO AND THE HYENA

This tale is about Hyena and Gizo. Gizo was afraid to meet up with Hyena because they did not get along. One day Gizo decided to go to the king's palace to greet the people there. Hyena asked, "Is it because you think you're cleverer than me that you're going to greet the king? What have I done wrong?" Gizo said, "You're a bad travelling partner because you're always doing shameful things. Shame doesn't mean anything to you. But okay, we'll travel together and try to settle our differences, so get ready to go." "Honestly Gizo I won't do anything like that," Hyena told him. "You won't?" "No," Hyena said.

Gizo said, "We can't go to greet the king empty-handed. Do you see the honey over there in that barrel? That's what I'm going to bring the king." So Hyena got some honey also. They each made a gammo and carried their goods on their heads.

They travelled for a long time together. Hyena began plotting and thought, "Why do I have to carry this honey all the way to the king? I refuse to take it to him. I'm going to trick Gizo. I'll eat all of the honey and defecate in the bottle."

After some time Hyena said, "Wait, I want to look around here. I'll be right back." Gizo said, "You're up to no good which is in line with your character." Hyena replied, "What do you mean I'm going to do something in line with my character?" Gizo looked for some shade to sit in while Hyena went behind a tree and ate all of her honey. Then she squatted and defecated diarrhea into the bottle. Flies followed her, and Gizo asked, "What's going on?" "Stop bothering me and let's go!" she told him.

They travelled for a long time until they reached the town. They arrived safely but met some cruel children who began yelling, "Hyena! Hyena! Ha!" A man saw them and thought, "These two must be looking for some place." They were shown the way to the palace where they unloaded their things.

Gizo said, "Long live the king! We live in the bush and decided we'd come to town." They told the king, "We've come to greet you." Gizo said, "As for me, here is what I've brought you. Open it, stick your thumb in and taste it." The king stuck his thumb in the barrel of honey, licked it three times and said that he wanted to keep it.

Hyena said, "Long live the king! Here's what I've brought." There were many flies around Hyena's bottle. Someone asked, "Why are all of these flies following this honey?" Hyena said, "Long live the king! Put your thumb in." The king stuck his thumb in and took it out. The smell was awful and the king got up. There were flies everywhere. Soap was brought to the king and he washed his hands. The king said, "Put this in the latrine."

Hyena and Gizo were given a place to stay and were brought meat and honey to eat. Hyena went to the bathroom while Gizo ate the food. He ate all that he could and put the rest into a sack. Then Gizo urinated and put some gravel and the urine in a bowl.

When Hyena returned she said, "Gizo, get up and let's eat." Gizo told her, "Oh, I can't eat because I have a stomachache." Hyena pulled the food toward her and scooped up some of the gravel and said, "Yuck!" "What is it?" Gizo asked. Hyena said, "What? Is this my food?" Gizo asked, "Is your food tough?" Hyena said, "Did I say that? I didn't say that! For God's sake don't tell the king I said that the food he gave us was tough. Please keep this a secret." Gizo watched her while Hyena ate the mixture of urine and gravel.

Time passed and soon they had spent seven days at the palace. Gizo said, "We should go to the bush and collect some stalks to give to the king." They went into the bush and began to collect stalks. Gizo had collected only a handful when he began yelling, "Oh God, my stomach! Oh God, my stomach!" He did this because he wanted to eat the remaining food that he had hidden in the sack. Gizo sat down and ate the food while Hyena continued to collect stalks.

After finishing all of the food he urinated and put some gravel and the urine in the sack and laid down. Hyena came and said, "Get up and let's eat, Gizo." Gizo said, "I'm not feeling well, and you want me to eat with you? My stomach is giving me problems." "Hey, this food is very tough," said Hyena. Gizo asked, "What did you say? They'll hear you." "I didn't say that. Please keep this a secret." Hyena ate the gravel and drank Gizo's urine and returned to collecting stalks.

Hyena worked and worked. She collected so many stalks that she had difficulty carrying her bundles, but she continued working. Gizo collected only two handfuls of stalks, tied them in a bundle and went to sleep.

When it came time to carry the loads to the king Hyena had to sit down so Gizo could tie them to her back. It was very difficult for her to travel. Gizo followed her with his small bundle on his shoulder.

They travelled until they were close to the town and Gizo said, "Give me your bundles and I'll help you." Gizo sat down and Hyena tied the bundles to his back. Gizo said, "Okay, take my small bundle the rest of the way." "Now I'm happy," Hyena said.

They travelled until they reached the door of the king's place where Hyena said, "Give me my bundles." Gizo told her, "Hyena, you're stupid. How could you have possibly collected all of this? Even if someone saw you with it they would know that I did all the work."

Gizo entered the palace and dropped his load of stalks. Someone said, "Congratulations Gizo!" Hyena said, "Liar! It wasn't him who collected them, it was me! They're mine!" Someone said, "Okay, go away, we've heard that it's yours." Hyena dropped her small bundle and someone came and took it.

Gizo told the king, "If God brings us to tomorrow we'll leave your town. You know we're people of the bush and unfamiliar with work in the town." Members of the king's court came and told Gizo, "We want to give you a gift. A rope used to tie a bull will be attached to a small goat, and a rope used to tie a goat will be attached to a bull. The ropes will appear from behind the house and you'll be told to choose one. If Hyena wants to choose first, let her."

Two ropes were thrown out, and Gizo was told to choose one. When he got up to choose Hyena interrupted, "Aren't I bigger than you? I'll choose first," and she grabbed the thicker rope. The rope she chose was attached to her gift and the goat was brought to her. Gizo was given a large, strong bull.

Gizo mounted the bull and Hyena mounted the goat, and they travelled for some time. It was because of Hyena's stupidity that she mounted the goat. Gizo rode his bull and when he got far ahead he stopped and waited for Hyena to catch up. Hyena began to get

23

angry and Gizo asked, "What's the problem? You have four legs and I have four legs to travel with." Hyena said, "Okay, let's go."

The goat started to give Hyena problems and screamed, "Baah!" Hyena said, "I know what you want. Three legs are better to travel with, three legs are better to travel with." Gizo asked, "How is it that four legs are not good to travel with? How can three legs be travelled on?" Hyena replied, "Is it your goat or mine?" Then she cut off a leg and ate it.

They continued travelling until the goat said, "Baah!" Hyena said, "Two legs are better to travel with," and she cut off another leg and ate it. A short time later she cut off the remaining legs and ate them. When she saw the goat could no longer walk she ate the rest of it.

When she realized that she did not have anything left she told Gizo, "We must slaughter your bull." Gizo agreed, but told Hyena to fart to keep the flies away while he slaughtered the bull. Hyena farted and flies came. When they got closer to Gizo's house they tried again. This time when she farted no flies came so they slaughtered the bull.

After the bull was slaughtered Gizo saw the setting sun was a bright red. He told Hyena to go and get some fire from the sun so that they could cook the meat. Hyena ran and ran but could not catch the sun. She became tired of running and returned. As she arrived Gizo had just finished butchering the bull and had put the meat high up in a tree. Hyena tried and tried to make him come down, but he refused.

Hyena went and asked Ostrich to come and help her. Ostrich tried and tried to make him come down, but Gizo refused. Ostrich got tired and told Hyena that she was going to eat her. When Hyena heard this she ran all the way back to her house. So from this time Hyena has been afraid of Ostrich.

# GIZO AND THE LIZARD

This tale is about Gizo and Lizard. One day in an isolated town there lived a king who had a beautiful daughter. They tried and tried to find a suitable husband for her but failed. They could not find a man she liked.

One day she announced that she would marry the man who could go to the fields and work from morning until night without drinking the juice of the dimniya. This was a difficult task because the juice of the dimniya is sweet and irresistible.

People heard the news of the king's daughter, but all those who came failed to marry her. People even came from faraway towns but were unsuccessful in their attempts to marry her. There were several men from the town who went to the fields and worked all day. But just as they finished their work they drank the juice of the dimniya. When they returned to town they said they had not drunk any. Then someone looked in their mouths and saw that they had drunk some.

One day Gizo heard the news of the king's daughter. If you know Gizo and that he heard about the king's daughter then you know how this tale will end. The quarrelsome and argumentative Gizo thought about how he could marry the king's daughter. He went home and prepared to go to the fields.

The next day Gizo went to the fields with a full water bottle and a stick and began to work. After he had worked for some time he went to the dimniya tree and picked some fruit. He drank and drank the juice until his thirst was quenched. Then he took his water bottle and rinsed his mouth out with water. He was careful to thoroughly rinse out his mouth. Then Gizo returned to town but forgot his water bottle in the fields. Although Gizo did not know, Lizard was watching everything he did.

When Gizo returned to town he went to the king's court and they looked carefully inside of his mouth. They announced that he had not drunk any juice of the dimniya, and he was married to the king's beautiful daughter.

After the wedding the king's daughter was taken to Gizo's house. After some time Lizard came and said, "Gizo, Gizo, you forgot your water bottle at the place where you drank the juice of the dimniya." Gizo said, "Oh Lizard, I didn't know you were close by, Lizard you have ruined the celebration this year."

Then a man from the king's court came and said, "We've heard what Lizard said." Lizard repeated, "Gizo, Gizo, you forgot your water bottle at the place where you drank the juice of the dimniya." Gizo said, "Oh, Lizard, I didn't know you were close by. You've ruined the celebration this year." The people went to the fields and saw that Gizo had indeed left his water bottle there. Then they returned home and the marriage was annulled.

## THE FULBE AND THE DODO

Once there was a Fulbe boy whose name was known in the north, south, east and west. There was also a girl who was the child of a man, but who was married to a dodo. This girl was skilled at braiding hair. She did it so well that no one could duplicate her work.

One day the boy, who was very self-confident, decided to go to the dodo's house to have his hair braided. He observed the dodo to learn his daily routine. When the dodo arrived with his animals, the boy hid among them and entered the compound. Once inside the dodo's compound the boy climbed a tree and hid.

When the boy arrived the girl was pounding millet. He broke off a twig and threw it into the millet. The girl picked it out. A short while later he broke off another twig and threw it into the millet. Again the girl picked it out. She said, "What is causing these twigs to fall into the millet? I'm pounding Dodo's millet. If it's a bird, fly away! If it's a man, come down quickly and tell me why you've come here. If my husband comes and finds you here you'll be his meat."

The boy came down and said, "It's a person." The girl asked, "How did you get in here without me seeing you?" "I snuck in," he told her. "Why have you come?" "The only reason I've come is to have my hair braided," he told her. "Braided?" she asked. "Yes," he said. "You want me to braid your hair while I should be pounding millet?" "Yes, exactly," he said. "Put aside your pounding and braid my hair." She told him, "This is a dodo's house. I'm the daughter of a man, but the head of this house is not a person!" The boy said, "I know that." Bera put aside her mortar and covered the millet.

The boy had come with his hair unbraided so she began combing it. She began to part his hair when she heard the dodo returning with his animals. When the dodo arrived home he always said something to let her know it was him, and she would answer him. He stopped at the door and said, "Bera pound for me, Bera grind for me, Bera pound quickly!" "Do you hear that?" the girl asked. "The dodo is coming!" The boy replied, "Let him come." Again the dodo said, "Bera pound for me, Bera grind for me, Bera pound quickly!" The boy who was lying down replied, "Here is a Fulbe hero who is preventing Bera from pounding and grinding, Bera braid quickly!" The dodo asked, "Is someone saying this from inside of my compound? Something is going to happen today." No one opened the door for him so he forced it open and went in.

He saw Bera sitting there. She was in the process of parting the boy's hair and had not yet began to braid it. The dodo stopped and said, "Bera pound for me, Bera grind for me, Bera pound quickly!" The boy replied, "Here is a Fulbe hero who is preventing Bera from pounding and grinding, Bera braid quickly!"

The dodo grabbed the boy, threw him in the mortar and began to pound him with the pestle. When he finished he took him out and spread him on the ground to dry. After some time the dodo saw that the boy had dried and said, "Bera pound for me, Bera grind for me, Bera pound quickly!" The boy responded, "Here is a Fulbe hero who is preventing Bera from pounding and grinding, Bera braid quickly!"

The dodo put the boy back into the mortar and pounded him again until he was powder and said, "Bera pound for me, Bera grind for me, Bera pound quickly!" But again the boy replied, "Here is a Fulbe hero who is preventing Bera from pounding and grinding, Bera braid quickly!"

The dodo made food out of the boy and took it out of the pot while the girl sat and watched. The dodo spoke and the boy again answered.

Then the dodo ate the food that he had made out of the boy. When he finished he went and defecated and said, "Bera pound for me, Bera grind for me, Bera grind quickly." From the bottom of the latrine the boy answered, "Here is a Fulbe hero who is preventing Bera from pounding and grinding, Bera braid quickly!"

The dodo said, "Bera?" "Yes Dodo," she replied. He asked, "Where did you find this boy?" "I had never seen him before until he came here," she said. "He told me to put aside my pounding and braid his hair. I told him that this was your house, but he said he didn't care." The dodo told her, "Quickly, braid his hair and send him on his way. This is not a man, he's a spirit. I pounded him, made him into powder, ate him, defecated him and he still spoke to me. Quickly braid his hair so that he can be on his way and leave our home." So the girl braided his hair.

The dodo was afraid and after the boy's hair was braided he said, "Take this camel and go!" The boy took the camel and left. On his way home he was not feeling well because of all that he had been through. Then he met another Fulbe who asked him, "Hey, where did you get your hair braided?" He said, "If you knew where I went to have this done you wouldn't be asking me." "Where did you have it done? Tell me how to get there so I can have my hair braided also." "You cannot go there," he warned him. "Why not?" the other Fulbe asked. "You went so why can't I go?" The boy told him, "The dance of two people is not the same. I suffered where I went to have this done. If you go you'll be killed." Again he asked, "You had your hair braided so why not me?" Finally the boy said, "Okay." He told him, "I went to the dodo's house. Bera did it for me at the dodo's house." "You went to the dodo's house to have your hair braided so why shouldn't I?" "Alright," the boy said. "I'll see your departure but not your return. You better go and say good-bye to your family because you'll never see them again."

The other Fulbe went to his parents and said, "I've seen a boy who had his hair braided beautifully at a dodo's house. Now I'm going to have it done." His parents warned him, "No, don't do what he did, you can't do what he did!" He asked, "What's the difference? He went so why shouldn't I?" His parents said, "We'll see you when you come back."

The boy went to the dodo's house. The other boy had told him how to get inside the compound and this boy did the same thing. Bera was pounding and the boy threw a twig at her. She said, "If it's the stranger from yesterday who has returned, if you aren't careful your days are going to come to an end." The boy came down from the tree and said, "It's not him. It's someone else who has come to have his hair braided." She asked him, "Do you know all of the suffering the other boy went through?" "Yes," he told her. She said, "Okay." "Put away your pounding and braid my hair," he told her.

The girl put down the pestle and prepared his hair to be braided. She was in the process of untying his current braids when the dodo came home. He arrived and said, "Bera pound for me, Bera grind for me, Bera pound quickly!" The boy replied, "Here is a Fulbe hero who is preventing Bera from pounding and grinding, Bera braid quickly." The dodo asked, "What? Has that fool returned or is it a different one? If it's the old one I'm not going into the compound until he has left. If it's a stranger I'll kill him."

The dodo went into the compound and saw that it was a different boy. He grabbed him, put him into the mortar and pounded him. When he finished he said, "Bera pound for me, Bera grind for me, Bera pound quickly!" The boy answered, "Here is a Fulbe hero who is preventing Bera from pounding and grinding, Bera braid quickly!" The dodo said, "This one is also stubborn. I think I'll leave him alone because I don't want to have something bad happen. I'll talk to him, and if he answers me I'll leave well enough alone."

The dodo put him back into the mortar and pounded him into powder. He squatted down and said, "Bera pound for me, Bera grind for me, Bera pound quickly!" The boy's voice was weaker but he replied, "Here is a Fulbe hero who is preventing Bera from pounding and grinding, Bera braid quickly!"

The dodo said, "Let me grind him up and make food out of him. If he still talks after that I'll leave him alone." He put the boy in a pot, stirred him, put the pot aside and said, "Bera pound for me, Bera grind for me, Bera pound quickly!" His voice even weaker, the boy replied, "Here is a Fulbe hero who is preventing Bera from pounding and grinding, Bera braid quickly!"

Finally the dodo said, "Let me go and defecate him. If he still talks to me I'll leave him alone." The dodo ate the food he made out of the boy, went and defecated him and said, "Bera pound for me, Bera grind for me, Bera pound quickly!" The boy replied, "Here is. . . a Fulbe. . . hero. . . . he is . . . . . preventing. . . . . . pounding. . . ."

## THE BOY WHO KILLED A DODO

Once there was a boy and a girl who lived with their mother and father. The family was wealthy, and farmed and kept animals for a living. God had blessed the husband and wife with children. The first born child was a girl. Time passed and the wife gave birth to a son. He was the last child and they spoiled him terribly. He was given everything he wanted no matter what it was. No one stopped him from doing what he wanted to do and in this way he grew up.

Time passed and one day the father became ill. After having been ill on and off for some time he called his wife and told her, "This illness hasn't responded to medication and I think I'm going to die from it." His wife began to cry and he told her, "Listen closely to the advice I'm going to give you. I don't have a mother, father or any relatives on my father's side of the family or my mother's side. They've all died. God has given us wealth and a family. If our two children behave poorly or you give them things that ruin their lives, don't worry because Paradise awaits us and God will judge all of us. I want you to give our son everything he asks for as I have done." The son heard all of this conversation. Then the father laid down and died a short while later. The period of mourning lasted for three days.

Time passed and the son behaved as usual because no one was permitted to discipline him. After some time the mother became ill. The daughter wondered who would plan her marriage if her mother died. At this time the boy was about twelve years old. Although he was a almost a teenager he still acted like a child.

The mother called her daughter and told her, "Now I have the illness that killed your father. It won't leave me. Look at you! You've grown into a beautiful woman. I won't be able to see your wedding, but by the grace of God you'll marry one day. The brother who your father entrusted us with must be obeyed because you're a woman. No matter what terrible things he does, you must obey him." The girl agreed and her mother died. That left only the girl and her brother in the house.

As time passed the boy behaved as before, and the girl stood by and did nothing. One day he said, "Sister!" She asked, "What is it little brother?" He said, "I want to light our cattle and camels on fire." She said, "Little brother . . ." He interrupted her and said, "Before mother and father died what did they tell you?" He took all of the animals and set them on fire. Then he burned all of their wealth and possessions except for the food.

The girl was no longer wealthy. She took some of the food and went and dug a big hole. She buried the food that she had taken in the hole.

One night he said, "Sister!" "What is it little brother?" she asked. He said, "I'm not satisfied. Now I want to set all of our granaries on fire." She said, "Little brother, don't you know that we store our millet there? You're going to burn all of our food." "It's none of your business!" he shouted. "Don't you remember what mother and father told you?" And he went and burned all of their granaries.

In the morning the girl went to where she had buried the millet. She took some of the millet, made breakfast and they ate.

One day the boy asked, "Where do you get the millet to make the fura and tuwo we eat?" "I go to town and work for it," she told him. "Okay," he said. The boy took some ash and put it in her back pocket. When she got up the next morning to get some millet she left a trail of ash leading to the place where she had buried it.

A week went by and the boy said, "Sister!" "What is it little brother?" "I want to burn the millet you buried in the hole," he told her. The girl was shocked and said, "Now . . ." He said, "Mother and father said . . ." "Go and burn it," she told him. He went and burned the millet leaving them with nothing to eat.

One day her brother said, "Sister!" "What?" she asked. "Are you going to burn me now?" "No," he told her. "We're going to leave this town." "Where are we going?" "Just get up, we're leaving!" the boy said.

They travelled until they came to a large town which stretched far to the north, south, east and west. In this town there were no people on the street at night. Not even a bird was out during this time because at night a dodo entered the town and wandered around until sunrise. After sunrise it was safe for people to come out again because the dodo had returned home.

When they reached the town they stopped in front of an old woman's house. The girl and the old woman greeted each other. The old woman asked, "Where do you come from?" "We're strangers," the girl told her. The old woman said, "If a stranger comes to our town they'll have many problems. If a stranger stays at my house and something bad happens in the town the king will blame me. Our town is nice but before nightfall everyone goes home and locks their doors." "Why?" asked the girl. "Because there's a dodo who comes to the town," the old woman explained. The girl said, "Now that I know about this dangerous thing why would I go out at that time?" "Okay, you can stay here," said the old woman. The girl said, "I have a little brother who's poorly behaved. If something happens to him I'll be happy to be rid of him." The boy was listening to the conversation while he was playing, but acted as if he did not hear them. Then he shouted, "Sister!" "What is it?" she asked. "Can we stay here?" "Yes," she told him, and they stayed at the old woman's house.

The boy went to the outskirts of town and came back dragging a stick which he left behind the old woman's house. Then he went out and picked some ripe fruit from a tree and prepared for the dodo's arrival.

Time passed but the boy did not return to the old woman's house. "Little brother, little brother! Where is my little brother?" cried the girl. He said, "Here I am outside." She said, "Come in, we're going to lock up the house." "Lock up!" he replied. "But aren't you coming in?" she asked. "It's none of your business!" he told her. She said, "If you're killed by the dodo it's not my fault." He told her, "Don't worry. If I die you won't be buried with me, and if you die you're not taking my life with you. Don't you remember what mother and father told you?" The girl said, "Old woman, let's lock up the house." And they went into the house and locked the door. Outside the boy lit a fire. The light from the fire could be seen from far away in every direction.

After some time the dodo came into the town. At this time not even a dog was on the street. When he entered the town the dodo asked, "Who is stronger than I in this town? Who is stronger than I, Dodo?" The boy answered, "I am stronger than you in this town! I am stronger! Me, Little Brother, I am stronger than you!" The dodo stopped and was furious. Never before had he been so angry. He thought, "Today someone in this town has answered me. Is there really someone stronger than I here?"

The dodo listened to find out where the voice was coming from. He entered the center of town and again asked, "Who is stronger than I in this town? Who is stronger than I, Dodo?" The boy replied, "I am stronger than you in this town! I am stronger! Me, Little Brother, I'm stronger than you!"

The dodo walked toward the boy and asked, "Who is stronger than I in this town? Who is stronger than I, Dodo?" The boy replied, "I am stronger than you in this town! I am stronger! It is I, Little Brother! I am stronger!" The dodo grabbed the boy, so the boy grabbed some fire and threw it at the dodo. But the dodo continued to hold on to him. Then the boy took some hot coals and stones and threw them at the dodo. After he did this the dodo fell down and died.

The old woman called out to the girl, "Where are you?" The girl said, "I'm over here. I'm happy now because my little brother is dead."

Meanwhile the boy had taken the dodo to the doorstep of the king's palace. He took off one of his sandals and laid it on top of the dodo and left. When he reached the old woman's house he crawled in under the door and fell asleep in the entrance room.

At dawn the muezzin came out and began the call to prayer, "Allah! . . ." When he saw the dodo he quickly went back into his house. The leader of the prayers said, "I heard the muezzin begin the call to prayer but he stopped. What happened?" He came out of his house from within the palace. When he opened the door of the palace he saw the dodo and quickly returned inside his house.

Women were on their way to the town well to draw water. To get to the well they had to take the main road which passed in front of the palace. As they passed the door of the palace they saw the dodo, dropped their water pots and ran home.

At about eight o'clock the king came out onto his balcony and asked, "Is all well in the town today?" He looked over the town, saw the dodo on his doorstep and said, "Things are not well! The dodo that prevents us from going out at night is now here during the day. It's no longer safe to go out at any time now!"

They summoned a brave man and told him, "There's trouble. There's a dodo at the front door of the palace, and we don't know if he's dead or just asleep. If he's alive there's nothing that we can do to stop him from sleeping here." The brave man was summoned and said, "Long live the king! I'll go and see if the dodo is dead or alive." He went and stood in front of the dodo. He inspected him and said, "Long live the king! This dodo is dead." The king replied, "You're lying!" The brave man said, "Long live the king! Look, he won't wake up even when I push him. Also, someone has left a sandal on him." Everyone was happy. The king announced, "We must find the person who has the other sandal because he is the one who killed the dodo!"

The king called all of the people of the town together. They were gathered so close together that someone could have suffocated. The king said, "I haven't called this meeting because of any wrongdoing. The person whose foot fits this sandal perfectly is the one who killed the dodo." Someone tried it on, but it was too big. Another tried it on, but it was too small. All of the people from the town and surrounding villages tried on the sandal, but it did not fit anyone's foot perfectly.

Someone in the crowd said, "There are two strangers staying at the old woman's house on the outskirts of town. We saw them, a boy and a girl." They went to the old woman's house. When the girl saw the crowd coming she was afraid. The boy asked them, "Are you going to kill us? Did we insult the king, or are we accused of killing someone? Why have you come?" The king explained, "We haven't come because of any wrongdoing. The person whose foot fits this sandal perfectly is the one who killed the dodo. We're looking for the owner of this sandal."

They told the boy to try on the sandal, but he refused. The king said, "Boy, I command you to try on this sandal. If it fits you perfectly you can't even begin to imagine the reward that will be yours." The boy took the other sandal out of his pocket, went to the dodo and laid it on top of him. The king looked at the boy and the boy looked at the king.

The king asked him, "What town do you come from?" The boy said, "Long live the king! I'm a stranger from a faraway town." The king asked, "A stranger from which town?" "That isn't important," the boy told him. "What is important is that God brought me here." The king said, "God brought you here to rid us of this terrible thing which has been terrorizing our mothers and grandparents? This horrible thing which has prevented us from going out at night? You came and rid us of this thing! As a reward I'm going to give you half of my kingdom to rule over. Also, you may choose one of my daughters to marry and I'll take your sister as my wife."

They returned to the old woman's house and a large celebration was held. The king married the boy's sister and she was taken to the palace. Also, the boy was given half of the town to rule over.

## THE CRUEL STEPMOTHER

This tale is about a man whose wife was unable to become pregnant. One day the husband said to his wife, "We've been together for a long time now, but God has not given us a child. I'll soon be middle-aged and without children, so I'm going to take a second wife so I may have a child. Maybe one day you'll also have a child." "I understand," his wife said.

The man married a second wife and shortly after her arrival she became pregnant. As soon as she became pregnant the first wife lost her status in the house. Then, by the grace of God, the first wife also became pregnant.

One day the second wife gave birth in the morning, and the first wife gave birth in the afternoon. All of the food in the house was secretly taken to the second wife's room. People came and the naming ceremony was held. The children grew, and soon the daughters of both wives became young women.

One day the first wife became ill and called her daughter. She told her, "You know that even while I've been alive things have been difficult for you in this house. Take my riches, dig a hole in the middle of our room and bury them. If you're allowed to stay in the room you'll have access to them. If you're not left in the room then you may return one day when you have matured and take these riches." A short time later her mother died leaving her to live with her half-sister, stepmother and father.

Every morning she was given a full mortar of millet to pound. If someone came to help her they were told not to by her stepmother. Every afternoon she was given guinea corn to eat by her half sister who stole the food and brought it to her behind the house.

The day of a large festival came and the girl did not know what to do. She washed her tattered clothes and got dressed. Then the girl had an idea and ran to her mother's grave. She was kneeling and crying next to her mother's grave when she noticed some soap, a body scrubber and some water. The girl took the water, soap and scrubber and went and bathed. When she returned to her mother's grave she found some makeup, jewelry and beautiful clothes. She put on the makeup and beautiful clothes and went to the festival. She wore earrings, necklaces and bracelets made of gold.

From the moment she arrived at the festival the king's son noticed her. He watched her and followed her everywhere she went. Her half-sister looked for her in the crowd. The king's son came up to her and asked her where she was from. She told him a faraway town. When the festival was almost over the girl left secretly. Before she left, the king's son had noticed that she had a large scar on a certain part of her body.

The girl returned to her mother's grave, left the clothes she had worn to the festival and put on her tattered clothes. After putting on her tattered clothes she returned to the festival. Her half-sister asked, "Where have you been?" The king's son came and asked the half-sister, "Who is this girl?" "This is my sister," she replied. The king's son took her aside and asked, "Was it you I saw earlier?" He told her that he wanted to marry her. She explained the difficult situation that she was in and he said, "Don't worry." He gave them some money and said, "Happy festival."

They returned home and the girl said, "Look at the money I received at the festival!" Her father and stepmother were surprised to see that someone had given her a gift. Her half-sister said, "Father, my sister has found a husband. The son of a king in another town is in love with her. Father, if you don't give her permission to marry him you're being cruel."

They discussed this in the morning, and that afternoon the king's courtiers arrived. They unrolled a mat and sat down. "Where is the head of the house?" the courtiers asked. Someone went and called the father who greeted the visitors. One of the courtiers said, "The king's son wants to marry the girl who wore the tattered clothes to the festival." Her stepmother interrupted, "No! You must mean my daughter." Her daughter came from inside the house and said, "No, it's not me." They agreed to the marriage and the wedding was held. But her stepmother did not give her a gift.

The girl went to her mother's grave and told her about everything that had happened. Her mother said, "Before you're taken to your new house come here and see me."

The girl was now even more beautiful. She was given perfume and many other gifts. Ten strong men were needed to carry all of her things to her new home. In the morning she unpacked all of the many different gifts she had received.

One day her stepmother said, "I'm going to see this girl's new house." When she arrived she was surprised and said, "Look at all these wonderful things!" When she returned home she asked her husband, "Did you really give all those things to your daughter?" Then she insulted him. "I didn't give them to her!" he told her.

The girl gave all of these wonderful gifts to her half sister. When the mother saw this she fell down and died. Now they are living like this and enjoying their lives.

# THE GIRL WHO MARRIED THE KING

Once there were some girls who took their animals to graze. One day they got lost and the king of that land summoned them to the palace. The king asked them, "Where is your town?" They told him that they did not know where their town was. The king demanded that each of them tell him what type of work they did.

One of the girls was named Taroro. She told the king that in her town she took the animals to graze. The other girls told him that they did housework. The king married them all and kept them in the palace.

Every morning Taroro took her animals and the town's animals into the bush to graze. One day while she was in the bush Taroro saw a watering hole with grass growing in it, so she led the animals to it. When she arrived at the watering hole she noticed a house. The house had everything in it including a bed. Taroro went to the water, bathed, put on makeup, got into the bed and went to sleep.

Late in the afternoon Taroro collected the animals and went back to town. Among the animals she had a ram who was the leader. On the way home the ram said, "During the rainy season it rains for God. During the dry season it rains for Taroro." When they entered the town all of the animals were thin except for Taroro's which were fat. Everyone was surprised.

One day some Fulbe came to let their animals drink with Taroro's at the watering hole, and they saw the house. They asked, "What is this house doing here?" One of the Fulbe tiptoed into the house while Taroro was sleeping, stole one of her sandals and took it to the king in the morning.

He said, "King, something in your land has surprised me. There's a place which never before had a watering hole. But now there is a watering hole which Taroro brings her animals to so they may eat and drink. You see her animals aren't thin like the others. There's nothing wrong with them. Next to this watering hole there's a house. I snuck into the house and took a sandal from it.

Somewhere in your kingdom is a person who has the matching sandal."

The king announced, "Today all of the shepherds from the town and surrounding villages must come to the palace." All of the shepherds came and gathered in front of the king. Their animals were with them making noise. The king asked, "Who among you has this type of sandal?" Taroro was at home in the palace crying because she had been prevented from taking her animals out to graze. "Who does this sandal belong to?" asked the king. "All of the shepherds must try it on. If a woman tries it on and it fits her perfectly she'll be my wife. If it's a man I'll give him half of my kingdom."

One of the shepherds tried on the sandal, but it did not fit. Another tried it on, but it did not fit him either. All of the men tried on the sandal, but it did not fit any of them perfectly. Then a woman tried it on, but her foot was too big.

Taroro and her ram were home crying together. Finally she was summoned to the palace. When she arrived she said, "Long live the king! Have I done something wrong?" He told her, "Try on this sandal." She came forward, put it on and it fit her foot perfectly. "Now you'll be rewarded," the king said. She told the king, "Your first wife always makes me and the other girls from my town work while she sits in her chair." The king said, "I agree." The first wife was displaced, and the king made Taroro his senior wife. Taroro now lives like this in the palace. The animals sit at home because there is no one to take them to graze.

## THE KING'S DAUGHTER WHO REFUSED TO MARRY

Once there was a young, unmarried woman who was very haughty. This haughty young woman, who was also the daughter of a king, would listen to no one. There were no other young women in the land as beautiful as her. Many men fell in love with her, but none of them had wealth great enough to offer her. She did not like any of her suitors.

One day a poor man came to see her and she said that she did not like him either. She told him it was not possible for her to live in the house of a poor man. Then a wealthy man came to seek her hand in marriage, and she refused him also. At this point the young men of the town gave up completely. She refused to even look at them let alone say that she liked one of them.

People in another town heard the news of this woman. The young men and boys of the town came to court her, but she did not like any of them. The news of this beautiful woman who refused to marry reached faraway lands. People from these lands packed their things and came to see her. The woman wondered what she was going to do with them since she did not want any of them to be her husband. Kings came from the north and the south seeking to marry her, but she refused all of them.

In a faraway town there lived a poor man. This man had always been poor and clothed himself with rags. His small house was like a chicken coop. He spent every day collecting grass to sell. He received a pittance for the grass and spent all the money to survive. In his town he went to the wealthy people who gave him food or a little money to spend. His poverty controlled his life.

One day he found a hiding place near the town meeting place where the men were talking about this woman. The men were wondering how one of them could marry her. They looked among themselves for a brave man to marry her. The poor man said, "I would have already married this woman if it weren't for my poverty!" "How would you have married her?" asked one of the men. "You don't understand women. I know what I'd do to marry her. If you give me the things I need I'll go and marry her and not return to this town until she has a baby or is pregnant. I'll bring her to you!" the poor man told them. "Really?" the men asked. "It's impossible!" said one man.

The men agreed to give the poor man everything he asked for and one year to marry and bring the king's daughter to them. The poor man said, "Be sure not to let the goats destroy my straw house and don't leave any of my things where they can be spoiled. Collect all my tattered clothes and put them in my house." "We'll do it," they told him. "Now what do you need?" The poor man said, "Load some camels with expensive perfume, kola nuts and incense. Also collect some black and white gowns for me and load them onto a camel. Finally, I need some traditional bracelets made of silver and gold." The men said, "Okay, consider it done. Remember if you don't marry the king's daughter and bring her here, no matter where you hide, we'll find you and kill you!" The poor man agreed, adding, "If I fail, you may kill me here in this public meeting place." The men collected all of the expensive things he had asked for. After he received them the man went and bathed. Then he loaded his things, mounted his magnificent horse and set off.

The man travelled for a long time before reaching the town. He stopped at the house of an old woman and said, "I'm just passing through. My animals and I would like a place to rest before continuing." The old woman said, "You can stay in that small shack over there." "That'll be fine," he replied. The old woman said, "Having a guest is a good thing!"

The man's things were unloaded and all put in one place. The horse was brought into the compound while the camels were led behind it. The man's horse stood alone in the middle of the compound. The man told the boy who worked for the old woman to bring his horse food before she woke up in the morning and to then sweep up the compound. The man had already watered his horse along the road, so when the old woman brought some water for the horse it would refuse to drink.

The man took some bottles of perfume, poured them into the water bowl and said, "Old woman, come and take the water that you brought my horse. He doesn't drink regular water, come and see the type of water he drinks. He has finished drinking, you may take the rest." "Perfume?" thought the old woman. She said, "This isn't water, it's perfume!" The man said, "This is what my horse drinks." The old woman began trembling. She took the perfume and kept it.

Then she brought the horse some food, poured it into his feed bag and left. The man took the millet out of the horse's feed bag, replaced it with kola nuts and said, "Old woman, my horse doesn't eat the type of food you brought. Come and see the type of food he eats." The old woman scooped out some of the food and saw it was the highest quality kola nuts. She began trembling again and took the leftover kola nuts.

The old woman brought some wood into the man's room to build a fire. The man said, "No, leave it there," and the old woman left. He put aside the wood that she had brought and took out some incense and kindling. He took four pieces of kindling and started a fire. When the fire began to burn the kindling he put it out. The incense began to burn and he put that out too.

In the morning the man told the old woman, "Come and clean the fireplace in my room." The old woman went and looked. She began to tremble as she cleared out the fireplace.

The old woman went to the king's daughter and said, "I have some good news for you! If you say that you don't want to marry the stranger who is staying at my house then there is no one acceptable to you in this world. If it is wealth that you want, come to the house of wealth!" The old woman took out the perfume and told the king's daughter, "This is the type of water his horse drinks!" She took out the kola nuts and said, "This is the type of food his horse eats!" She took out the remnants from his fire place and said, "This is the type of wood he uses to build a fire!"

The king's daughter made some food and told her servant, "Take this food to the guest at the old woman's house." The man ate the food and filled the bowls with gold coins. He also filled straw baskets with silver and said, "Old woman, take these things to the king's daughter."

When the old woman gave the gifts to the king's daughter she prayed to God for the sunset to come so she could go and visit the man. When darkness fell the king's daughter put on her best clothes and left. She went and met the man at the old woman's house. She entered his sweet-smelling room which smelled so good that she could not identify all of the odors. The man was wearing a black and white gown, and they chatted for a long time.

After she left, the man took a woven blanket and filled it with gold and silver coins and said, "Old woman, take this to the king's daughter." When the king's daughter returned home she told her father that she had found the man she wanted to be her husband. She told him that if she could not marry this man that she did not know who she would marry. Her father said, "Wonderful! We have waited for you to find a suitable husband. Let's plan the marriage!"

The man was married to the woman, and they celebrated at the old woman's house. The old woman's servant was sent to announce the marriage to the townspeople and everyone enjoyed themselves.

Time passed and soon the king's daughter gave birth to a son who in time began to crawl. One day the man went to the king and said, "I've married here and now have a son. I must go and visit my family." The king said, "You're right. Since you have family you should go and visit them." Servants came and prepared for their departure. Slaves were brought to accompany the king's daughter and all of her belongings. The algaita was played at her departure.

When they arrived at the outskirts of town the man gave the order to stop. He told them that he was going into town to tell his family to get everything ready and that he would send someone to come and bring them to the public meeting place. He told them not to go into town alone, mounted his horse and rode into town.

The man had sent a message telling the people of his town the day he was coming home. The young men of the town were gathered at the public meeting place. The man told them, "Today the bet is over. My wife is coming with my son. I see you've taken care of my belongings, my house and my tattered clothing." He put on his tattered clothes and went and quietly sat in the doorway of his old house.

The king's daughter and the people who had accompanied her arrived at the public meeting place and asked, "Where is the groom's house? Where is the groom's house?" Someone asked, "Which groom?" Another person told them, "There it is." They looked into the house and asked, "Is it really him?" The poor man said, "Yes it's me! Here's my house and my belongings." The king's daughter looked at him from atop her horse and said, "Throw him his son." Someone threw the poor man his son, and she said to the others, "Let's return home." "Your reputation is finished! Your haughtiness is finished!" he shouted after her. "The young men of our town came seeking to marry you, but you refused them all. Now you see my true home here." The king's daughter left her belongings and returned home.

## THE GIRL WHO SAVED THE KING'S SON

Once there was a girl who lived with her family. The girl's mother died, and she was left to live with her stepmother and half-sisters. Whenever something was being shared by the family she was not given any; she simply sat alone by herself. She was well-behaved and did everything her father told her to do no matter what it was.

Every week her father travelled to markets in different towns to trade. Whenever he was about to go to the market all of the children told him what to bring them, except for the girl, who never asked for anything.

One day she had some coins and gave them to her father so he could buy her some bean cakes when he went to the market. Although she had never asked him for anything before, on this day she had the good fortune of having some spare change and asked her father to bring her something. She waited for all the other children to ask for what they wanted before she made her request.

Her father took the money and went to the market. When he arrived there he did all of his trading and bought the things he needed as well as the things his children had asked for. By the time he finished trading it was afternoon.

When he was about to leave the market he felt a small bundle of coins in his pocket. He took out the bundle of coins and saw the money that his daughter had given him. He remembered that she had asked him to buy her some bean cakes. He looked everywhere but could not find any. The man shouted, "Where can I find a bean cake seller? Where can I find a bean cake seller?"

It just so happened that Bean Cake was the name of the king's son, and it was forbidden for anyone to call out his name. A large group of the king's courtiers came and caught the man. They took him to the king's court and asked him why he was calling out the name of the king's son. He was asked, "Do you want to cause problems?" The man explained, "I have a daughter whose mother is dead. Whenever I go to the market she never asks me for anything. It was only today, after all the other girls told me what they wanted, that she asked me to buy her some bean cakes."

The men of the king's court let him go, and the king's son gave the man some bean cakes to take to his daughter. He also told him that he would come and visit his daughter on Friday. The man thanked him heartily. When he arrived home he gave his daughter the bean cakes and told her that the king's son was coming to visit her on Friday.

On Friday morning the girl cleaned her room and put all of her things in order. In the afternoon the king's son arrived and sat on the pointed roof of her house. The girl asked him to come in, and they spent a long time chatting. When he was about to leave he began to spit. Every time he spit, he spit gold. The girl collected her gold, put it in a safe place and the king's son left.

The king's son visited the girl every Friday. The girl's stepmother was unhappy and jealous that the king's son came every Friday to visit her step daughter. Early in the morning of the following Friday the stepmother placed some sharp thorns on the top of the girl's room. She did this because she knew that the king's son always sat on top of it before he went inside.

When the king's son sat on the thorns he was angry. The girl asked him to come in. He went in, but every time he spit only blood came out. When he returned home he could not walk well, talk or do anything. The next Friday he did not visit the girl.

The following morning the girl shaved her head, took a small bowl and a drinking gourd and set off for the town where the king's son lived. The girl travelled for days, resting and sleeping here and there.

One day she came to a large tree as night fell and slept there. In the morning she heard some birds singing, "You've heard that the king's son is not well. No one is pounding millet, no one is seeking alms. Everyone has tried their medicine, but nothing has worked. If someone takes our excrement, mixes it with water and gives it to him to drink, he'll get better." The girl heard the birds' advice, collected some of their feces and left.

The girl, disguised as a boy, took her bowl into the town and began to beg. The king's courtiers shouted at him, "The king's son is ill, and you've come into town to beg? Go away and leave us alone." She told them that she wanted to see the king's son to give him some medicine.

48

The king gave her permission to see his son. She asked that some hot water be brought quickly, so one of the king's wives lit a fire and put a pot of water on. When it began to boil they gave it to the girl. She added the bird feces to the water and poured some into the boy's mouth, and he drank it. After sleeping for a while the king's son sat up and began talking to people. Soon after he began walking again.

One day the girl told them that she was going home, and the king rewarded her with many riches. She set off with the king's courtiers and son accompanying her.

When they were far off in the bush the girl said she wanted to talk to the king's son alone. The others left them and they chatted. The king's son asked her, "What do you want me to give you from this town?" The girl told him that she did not want anything except for his ring. "Also, no matter what anyone does to you, if the person says, 'Leave me because of the beggar boy' then be patient and leave them alone." The king's son said, "Okay," and the girl returned home. She had left home secretly, so no one knew she had been gone.

On Friday the king's son arrived at the girl's house and went into her room with a large sword. She greeted him but he refused to answer her. As she was weaving he cut her thread, but she did not say anything to him. The second time he did it she said, "Leave me because of the beggar boy." The king's son was surprised and asked her, "Where did you hear about the beggar boy?" He cut the thread a third time and she said the same thing. He told her, "Even if you say that, I'm going to kill you." He drew his sword and she showed him the ring. "Who gave you this ring?" he asked. She said, "It was I that you spoke with in the bush. I was the beggar boy." And she told him the whole story.

The king's son returned home and told his parents that he wanted to marry the girl. They asked, "You want to marry the girl who tried to kill you?" He told them what had happened, and his father organized the marriage. The girl kept the gold that he spit and today they live together like this.

## THE GIRL WHO MARRIED A SNAKE

Once there was a beautiful girl who lived with her parents. She had older as well as younger sisters, and they lived an affluent life. In addition to being wealthy she was also very friendly.

One day a man came seeking her hand in marriage, but she refused him. Others followed and she refused them also. Then the girl announced, "I'll tell you who my husband will be. The man who has no scars on his body, not even one shall be my husband. If he has scars I won't marry him, but if he doesn't have any scars I'll marry him." A man came, but the girl found a scar on his body. Another came and she searched him, found a scar and refused to marry him.

Time passed. Then two brothers who were snakes heard about this girl and said, "One of us must marry her." The brothers travelled for several days until they reached the girl's town. When they arrived they stopped at an old woman's house to spend the night. The brothers said, "We've heard about the girl, and we've come to marry her." The old woman told them, "You know that this girl wants a handsome husband who has no scars." "May God give us the chance," said the brothers.

These two brothers were popular and they were known everywhere. Everyone who saw them said that the girl would marry one of them because of their beautiful, smooth skin. The snakes went to the girl to be searched for scars, and the younger brother was examined first. He failed because of a small scar he had from where a thorn had pierced his skin. The girl said she would not marry him. Then the older brother stepped forward and the girl looked at him. She examined him closely from head to toe but did not find a scar. She spent days examining his body looking for a scar but did not find one. She went to her mother and father and told them that she had found the man she wanted to marry. "No!" they told her. "Don't do something foolish like this. Once you leave here

50

your life will be terrible." The girl replied, "No matter what you say he is going to be my husband."

People came to the wedding, and the girl was married. Children from the town helped prepare for the wedding and the celebration. It lasted for two days and was enjoyed by everyone. The young couple was given a house to live in, and the girl was content with her husband. She also had the respect of her younger sister.

One day the husband said, "I came here and took a wife, but the only one to see the wedding from my family was my younger brother. I want to take my wife who I love so much to meet my family. After our visit we'll return here. We don't need to take anything with us because I have everything we'll need at my house. Give our possessions to her younger sister if she gets married before we come back."

The girl's parents told her younger sister, "We don't even know the name of the town where they are going so we want you to follow them." She agreed to follow them. Her parents told her, "You must make your own decisions during your visit."

She went and told her older sister, "I'm coming with you." "You're not coming! You'll destroy my marriage!" replied her older sister. The younger sister insisted that she follow them. The parents said, "Leave your younger sister alone. She'll go with you because there you won't have a mother or a father to take care of you. If you get sick or something happens to you your younger sister can come and tell us." They argued about this for some time. The younger sister repeated that she would follow her older sister. Finally the older sister said, "If you insist on following me then I'll kill you!" She lit her younger sister on fire with a match and watched her burn. Then she collected her ashes and scattered them.

The older sister, her husband and his younger brother prepared to leave. As they were leaving the younger sister's ashes turned into a fly and landed on her older sister. They travelled for some time with the younger sister attached to her older sister.

After some time they stopped and the husband asked, "Are you familiar with this part of the bush?" "Yes," his wife answered. "Sometimes we collect firewood here." Later he again asked, "How about this part of the bush?" "Yes," she told him. "We've been coming here since I was a child." The two brothers took her far into the bush until they asked her, "Are you familiar with this part of the bush?" and she said that she was not. The younger sister, who was still hanging on to her older sister, was memorizing the road they were following.

They continued travelling until they came to the husband's town. As they entered the town the younger sister made her presence known by transforming herself back into a person and announcing, "I've followed you!" Her sister threatened to kill her again, but her husband said, "Leave her alone. If a member of my family likes her you can give her to him in marriage. Your younger sister has come with us to help you, and you say that you don't want her here?" They arrived in the town and everyone greeted them. The sisters saw what they thought to be many people and a large town. But it was not really a town, and the people were not really people.

That night the older sister slept while her younger sister stayed awake. After some time the older sister's father-in-law came into the room saying, "Saima, saima dadis. Saima, saima dadis." The younger sister asked, "Who is it saying, 'Saima, saima dadis. Saima, saima dadis.'?" He answered, "It's your father-in-law saying, 'Saima, saima dadis. Saima, saima dadis.'" "What do you want?" she asked him. "I want some water. That's why I said, 'Saima, saima dadis. Saima, saima, dadis.'" "Come in and take some water," she told him. "But stop saying, 'Saima, saima dadis. Saima, saima, dadis.'"

He went over to the water pot, pretended to take some water and left. After that her mother-in-law came and did the same thing. The younger sister did not sleep a wink. Her older sister slept well that night because she was unaware of what was happening.

The next morning the younger sister said, "You're a fool! If you stay here you'll see what I saw last night. Your husband isn't a man, he's a snake!" "You're lying!" shouted her older sister. "Okay, tonight stay awake with me and you'll see."

That night every time the older sister fell asleep her younger sister shook her. The girl's father-in-law came into their room saying, "Saima, saima dadis. Saima, saima dadis." The older sister was afraid and grabbed her younger sister who told her, "Wait, you'll see that what I told you is true." Then she asked, "Who is it saying, 'Saima, saima dadis. Saima, saima dadis?'" He answered, "It's your father-in-law saying, 'Saima, saima dadis. Saima, saima dadis." She asked, "What do you want? Why are you saying, 'Saima, saima dadis. Saima, saima dadis?'" "I want some water. That is why I've come saying, 'Saima, saima dadis. Saima, saima dadis.'" "Come in and take some water but stop saying, 'Saima, saima dadis. Saima, saima dadis.'"

He came into the room, pretended to take some water and left. The older sister's mother-in-law came and did the same thing. Her brother-in-law and husband followed and did the same thing. The older sister said, "Oh God! We must escape or we'll surely die!" The younger sister told her, "Don't worry, you're not dead yet."

During the day the younger sister took fura to those working in the fields. One day, after delivering the fura, she climbed the highest tree she could find and sat quietly. On the ground beneath her she saw the husband and his younger brother turn into snakes and begin playing. From high in the tree the younger sister said, "Hello, young men of the town!" One of the snakes looked up but did not see her. Then he saw a dove and said, "Hello, little bird! When we eat the sisters we'll give you the thighs." When they had finished playing they became men again, dug a whole and buried the fura in it.

The situation remained like this for some time. One day the younger sister said, "Older sister, come with me. Today you'll see that your husband and his brother are not men as you think." The older sister said, "Okay."

When they arrived at the fields they climbed the same tall tree. The younger sister tied her older sister to a branch to prevent her from falling out of the tree when she saw the truth. The younger sister said, "Hello, young men of the town!" They answered, "Hello, little bird! When we eat the sisters we'll give you the thighs." "Did you hear that? You heard what they'll do with your own ears!" exclaimed her younger sister.

"How are we going to escape?" asked the older sister. "We'll run away!" she told her, and they returned home.

The older sister lost her appetite and became thin. She spent most of her time crying. The younger sister said, "You said you wanted to marry him! The day I decide to run away I'm leaving. I'll leave you here for them to eat!" The older sister began crying even louder until her husband came and asked, "What is making her cry?" The younger sister said, "I don't know why she's crying. Why don't you ask her?" The husband spoke with his wife.

Time passed and the sisters were well-taken care of so they could be eaten. One day the younger sister said, "Today we're going to run away if we have the chance. If they want to eat us they'll have to eat us on the road." That day they decided to run away. The younger sister said, "I want you to bring some wet sand, a shield and some charcoal. I'll bring some other things." The older sister agreed.

That afternoon the younger sister said, "It's time to take your husband and his brother their lunch in the fields." They took them their lunch in the fields. On their way home they said, "May the road give us luck," and began their escape. They ran and ran as fast as they could.

Back at the house the husband's father asked, "Is all well in our home today?" "What could be wrong?" replied his wife. The husband's younger brother was called to make sure that everything was alright. When he arrived he searched high and low for the sisters but could not find them. He asked his father, "There's no one else in the house? No one at all?" "That's right," his father told him. The brothers asked, "What can we do?" Then they said, "We must follow them!"

The brothers chased the sisters through the bush. After some time the younger sister decided to look back to see if anyone was following them, and she saw the brothers. She told her sister, "They're following us!"

The brothers continued to chase them. Along the way the brothers stopped and turned into snakes. When she saw this the younger sister said, "Touch this tree stump." When her older sister touched it she became a tree stump with a mouth, nose and breasts. The younger sister turned into a fly and sat on the tree stump. The parents of the brothers who were helping with the chase said they were tired. They told their sons, "Go on without us and find your wife!"

The two brothers arrived at the tree stump. The younger brother said, "This tree stump is them!" "You're lying," said the older brother. "It's them! Have you ever seen a tree stump with a mouth and nose?" "You're right," agreed the older brother. "But how are we going to cut this tree stump when we don't have an axe? Go home and get something to cut it with." "I'm not going alone. We have to go together," replied the younger brother. So the two brothers went home to get an axe.

After they left the younger sister said, "Come on, let's go!" And they began running again. When the brothers came back to cut the tree stump they saw that it was gone. They asked, "How could a tree stump with a mouth, nose and breasts disappear?" "Well let's not sit here all day talking about it, let's follow them!" said the younger brother, and they ran and ran.

The younger sister again turned around to see if they were being followed. When she saw the snakes she told her sister, "Drop the shield!" When her sister dropped the shield it became a dense forest. By the time the brothers cut through the forest the sisters were again far ahead of them.

They continued running. The younger sister looked back again and saw the brothers getting close. She yelled, "Drop the charcoal!" Her older sister dropped the charcoal and a fire started in the bush. The snakes had to stop and put out the fire. They fought the fire until it was completely dead.

Meanwhile the sisters continued running. They were close enough to the town to see their house, but the snakes had again almost caught up to them. The younger sister looked back, saw the snakes chasing them and said, "Drop the wet sand!" Her sister dropped the wet sand and a river was created between the sisters and the snakes. She looked back and saw that the snakes had stopped. The snakes said, "We must become men to swim across the river." They changed into men and swam across the river.

While the brothers were crossing the river the sisters reached home. The younger sister told the story of what had happened to them.

Shortly after that the two brothers arrived and said, "Hello!" The younger sister told her parents, "Give them a room." After the brothers retired to their room she said, "Tonight everyone stay awake and listen. I want you to hear what they say and you'll see that they are really snakes. All of you arm yourself with a stick so we can kill them. If we don't do this they'll come back."

The brothers were given a lot of food, and everyone chatted for a while. They discussed the reasons that the wife had left her husband. The older sister's husband asked, "Why would we want to harm them? We were worried about her. We thought something may have eaten her in the bush."

The father told them, "Wait and let them rest. Then they can return with you. As for now I'm an old man who must go and work his fields." The brothers said, "Okay. We'll wait because they want to visit with you. When they've finished we'll leave."

The younger sister stayed awake to protect them from the two snakes. In the middle of the night they heard, "Saima, saima dadis. Saima, saima dadis." The younger sister asked, "Who is saying, 'Saima, saima dadis?'" The older sister's husband said, "It's your father-in-law who is saying, 'Saima, saima dadis. Saima, saima dadis.' I want some water. That's why I've come saying, 'Saima, saima dadis. Saima, saima dadis.'" "Come in and take some water," she told them. "But stop saying, 'Saima, saima dadis. Saima, saima dadis.'"

He came in to get some water and she said, "Hello, young men of the town!" He answered, "Hello, little bird! When we eat the sisters we'll give you the thighs." Then there was a commotion as everyone came running asking, "Who is saying these things?" The two brothers had turned into snakes. The people, who had already armed themselves with clubs, beat the snakes to death, bam, bam, bam!

## THE MAN AND HIS TWO WIVES

Once there was a man who had two wives. Everyone knows that if a man has two wives he will always favor one over the other. Time passed, but neither of his two wives bore him any children. Then his less favored wife gave birth to a baby girl. More time passed and the favored wife gave birth to a baby boy.

His love for his favored wife and their son was never-ending. He acted as if his less-favored wife was not even in the compound. The favored wife and their son received everything they wanted.

Every morning during the rainy season the man told his less-favored wife, "Get up! It's time to go work in the fields!" While the favored wife stayed home and cooked the food, the less-favored wife had to spend the whole day in the fields. She worked just as hard as her husband did there. At sunset he would tell her to collect firewood and return home. When she arrived home she had to husk the millet and do other chores. After this she was free to rest. When the sun rose the following morning, she would go to the fields and begin working again.

She lived this difficult life until one day she became ill. Her husband thought she was only pretending, so he continued to order her to go to the fields until she was unable to walk. During this time her daughter came to be with her. She took care of her mother by bringing her food and water. But her mother did not get better, and her condition worsened.

One day while the others were working in the fields she died. The daughter brought water for her mother. She called her mother repeatedly but heard only silence. She shook her, but there was no reply. The girl ran and told a neighbor, "My mother, I called to her but she didn't respond! I shook her but she didn't move!" They went and saw that her mother was dead. Then they went to the fields and told her husband who returned home. People came for her funeral, and she was buried.

Now the situation will be even more difficult for the girl. The girl's name was Zariya and the boy's name was Harouna. Every day Zariya and Harouna took the animals to graze. Zariya was given many chores to do which kept her busy from morning until night, at which time she had to go and collect the animals from grazing. She had to draw water from the well, pound millet and prepare fura.

One day Zariya and Harouna went to collect the animals from grazing. While they were gone the favored wife poured fura into a calabash bowl for them. She also put poison in the fura. Zariya, however, was protected by God.

On her way to collect the animals she stopped at her mother's grave and greeted her several times. Then, from the grave, her mother said, "Be careful when you go home. Harouna's mother has poisoned your fura. If Harouna drinks some you may drink some. If Harouna doesn't drink any then don't you drink any."

When Zariya and Harouna returned home they tethered all of the animals. Harouna's mother told Zariya, "Your fura is ready, come and get it. Take it over there and eat it." Zariya said, "Harouna, let's go and have some fura." "You can't eat it with him," his mother said. "That's for you." Harouna did not eat any of the fura, so Zariya took it behind the granary, dug a hole and buried it. She returned the calabash bowl and left it. Then she went to a neighbor who gave her something to eat.

At night Harouna slept on one side of the bed, his mother in the middle and Zariya on the other side. One day the favored wife told her son, "During the night I want you to nudge me and I'll push Zariya into the fire."

On her way to collect the animals Zariya stopped at her mother's grave and greeted her. Her mother told her, "I want you to switch places with Harouna's mother tonight."

That night while everyone was asleep Zariya switched places with Harouna's mother. When Harouna woke up he nudged Zariya and she pushed Harouna's mother into the fire. As she fell, the mother yelled, "It's me Harouna! It's me Harouna!" But it was too late, and she fell into the fire.

The next morning they woke up and shouted, "Mother has fallen out of bed!" Their father came running and stood next to the fire where the remains of his wife rested. "How did this happen?" he demanded. "Harouna, how did this happen? Zariya, how did this happen?" "I don't know," Zariya replied. "Mother made a fire," Harouna said. "She told me to nudge her during the night and that she would push Zariya into it." "How did this happen?" he again asked Zariya. She told him, "I don't know. I only know that she fell out of bed." Now the favored wife is dead and only Zariya, Harouna and their father are left.

Time passed and Zariya and Harouna were always together. Every day Harouna tried to devise a plan to kill his half sister.

One day, as usual, Zariya went to her mother's grave early in the morning to find out what was going to happen that day. Her mother told her, "Today don't eat or drink anything from your house. Harouna has put poison in it."

When Zariya returned home she tethered all of the animals. Harouna saw that she was not going to drink any water or eat any food so he took all of the water and poured it out except for one pot which he forgot. Since there was no water in the house Zariya and Harouna went out to get some.

In the morning Harouna drank water from the pot he had forgotten to empty the night before and died. This left Zariya to live with her unloving father alone. She now had the wealth and possessions of her mother, Harouna and her stepmother.

## THE BOY AND HIS SISTER

Once there was a warlike man whose name was known everywhere. There was also a king named Marmargu who was feared by everyone. When he attacked a town he reduced it to gravel before he would stop the attack. If he did not see that the town had been totally destroyed he was not content. He was content only when he saw that nothing was left of the town. This man had a horse which used to belong to King Marmargu.

Time passed and the man's wife gave birth to their first child, a daughter. The man said, "I wanted a boy who could go to war, but I don't reject the gift God has given me." When the man's daughter stopped nursing, his wife gave birth to a baby boy. Time passed and the boy grew. Everyone knows that when a boy is about seven years old he begins to be clever.

One day the man told his son about a war in a distant land which was twelve kingdoms away from their own, in the land of King Marmargu. The boy listened intently to what his father told him.

Time passed and one day the boy's father became ill. He called his wife and told her, "I've never been this ill before, perhaps I'll die. I'll leave you children without a father. We don't know whether we'll live longer than them or them longer than us, but please give them everything they ask for. Give all of the animals to our daughter, but the horse can only be ridden by our son. Take good care of our children." A short while later the father died.

The boy went to where his horse was tethered, cleaned the area and brought it some straw. He took good care of the horse because it was his most important possession.

Time passed and their mother became ill. She called her daughter and told her, "Some days I feel fine and others I don't. You must respect your younger brother. One day he'll provide for you if you treat him well. But if you treat him poorly you'll suffer and probably become a servant for someone. Your brother will provide everything." After giving her daughter that advice the mother died leaving only the brother and his sister.

This girl was irresponsible and did not do her housework. Her chickens pecked her brother on the back and he asked her, "Didn't you hear what our mother and father said? You're a woman, you must do your chores. But now I'm the one doing them! One day I'm going to leave, and we won't meet again until Paradise or until the day that God wills us to meet." "Where will you go?" she asked him. "I'm going to the land that father told me about."

Then one day he told her, "Good-bye. I'm going to tell our king that I'm leaving. If I come back, fine. If I don't that's that," and he went and told the king. The king asked, "Boy, how can you do this? It was because of Marmargu's warlike nature that your father left his kingdom. When he left Marmargu gave him this horse. If you go to his town it's not only you that they'll kill, they'll come here as well." The boy said, "I'm acting independently. I'm going alone, so it's me they'll blame." "May God give you luck," the king told him.

The boy loaded up his horse with as much as it could carry. He travelled until he arrived at a large, walled city and said, "When my mother died she left my sister, Tassala, chickens. Me, she left a horse to ride. I told Tassala that her chickens annoyed me. I accepted this, I accepted this, my sister. My mother came from Paradise and asked, 'Why do you accept that? Why do you put up with that, you who own Marmargu's horse, Marmargu the one who leaves towns in rubble?' It is he I am looking for, let him come out so I may see him. If he can fight, let him come and take back his horse. If I can fight better than he, I'll take his town."

The king of this town told the boy that he must leave immediately. "This isn't King Marmargu's town," he told him. He said that even if the boy spent the afternoon in the town he would not be allowed to spend the night.

The boy moved on and travelled deep into the bush and spent the night there. When he awoke he travelled until he came to another large town. He looked around the center of town and repeated what he had said. When the king of the town heard this he summoned the boy.

The boy went to the king and dismounted his horse. He looked at the king, and the king looked at him. The king asked, "Do you know the importance of what you are saying? Do you or don't you?"

61

The boy answered, "Well, I don't know the importance of it, but I heard my father say it." The king asked, "Where's your father?" "He's in another town," the boy replied. "And you took the horse? Where's your father?" asked the king. "He's dead," the boy told him. "You said you're going to King Marmargu's town. It's a long distance away. If you go there you won't survive," the king said. The boy told him, "Your highness, I'm going today because I've made my decision." "May God be with you," the king said.

The boy went to the next town but was chased away. At the following town he was given a place to stay. This was the town before King Marmargu's. It was the town of an old king who did not have any children. The king told the boy, "I want to tell you that you can't defeat King Marmargu. You've passed through ten towns. Mine is the eleventh. In all of the kingdoms there isn't anyone willing to fight against him. We don't want to fight him. We can't fight him today or tomorrow because he's not Muslim, and his methods of fighting are evil. Because you're brave and I'm an old man please stay here with me." The boy replied, "Your highness, I've made my decision to go. Whether I live or die is not important, I'm going. If I defeat him or he defeats me, the work of a man is always difficult."

The king gathered all the malamai of his kingdom and prayed to God to help the boy. The boy said, "If we meet again that's fine, but if we don't that's that." The boy mounted his horse and the king told him, "As you approach Marmargu's town there's a field. After that you'll come to a large tree near the gate of the palace. If it's not night you'll see the king."

The boy arrived in King Marmargu's kingdom armed with a sword, spear and shield. When he arrived the king was there with his men. The boy said, "When my mother died she left Tassala chickens. Me, she left a horse to ride. I told Tassala her chickens annoyed me. I accepted this, I accepted this. My mother came from Paradise and asked, 'Why do you accept that? Why do you put up with that, you who own Marmargu's horse, Marmargu the one who leaves towns in rubble?' It is he I am looking for, let him come out so I may see him. If he can fight, let him come and take back his horse. If I can fight better than he, I'll take his town."

As the king's men approached him the boy waved his arm and twenty of them fell down. "Wait!" the king shouted. "This isn't a man, it's a spirit! Wait, let's ask him some questions." The king asked, "Where are you from?" and the boy told him. "Who is you father?" And again the boy answered the king. "My mother and father are dead. Only my sister and I are left." The king said, "Rest and drink some water." But the boy told him, "I haven't come to drink your town's water! I've come to fight!" The king said, "Get down off of your horse and rest." The boy dismounted his horse and said, "Rest? No! If someone comes to fight why wait? If someone brings you food and you're hungry are you going to wait to eat?"

The war drums were sounded and the town thundered. They went to the battle field and fought for seven days. The boy fought the largest and strongest of the king's men first, and then the king himself. The king tired and said, "Let's rest," but the boy refused. They fought the whole afternoon and into the night and for another day until a week had passed. The seventh day the king said, "Let's rest." But again the boy said, "No," and knocked the king to the ground and stabbed him. The boy whistled for his horse and left.

The boy was made king of Marmargu's town, and his sister joined him. This is why if a stranger comes to your town don't chase him away because you don't know what he is capable of.

## THE BOY WHO MARRIED THE KING'S WIFE

Once there was a wife of a famous king whose name was known in the north, south, east and west. After she married the king a servant attended to her every need. Even the king did whatever she told him to do. If she told him not to go to visit his courtiers he would not go because he loved her very much. All of the townspeople talked about this girl.

It was God's will that a boy in another town heard about her. In his town there were many girls who liked him. His father told him, "Choose a girl and I'll take care of the wedding preparations," and his mother agreed. But the boy told them, "Not now. The woman that I marry must be famous."

Word spread quickly, and the news of the king's wife reached their town. They learned that the young men of her town were unacceptable to her, so the king of the town had married her. The boy listened to everything that people said about the girl.

When he went home his older sister suggested that he go to her town and talk with her. The boy decided that he must marry her. If he could not marry her then he would steal her away from the king and bring her back to his town.

The next morning he told his sister, mother and father, "Please forgive me, but I'm going to travel and see the world." His father said, "Wait, I'll give you a wedding here!" The boy said, "Don't you understand? I've never suffered, I'm naive. I only know the comforts of life. If you disappeared I would suffer because I don't know how to take care of myself. If I travel into the world and experience it I'll be able to take care of myself."

He collected all of the things he would need, got dressed and left town. Shortly after his departure he met up with Dodger. Dodger dodged here, dodged there and asked, "Hey, where are you going?" "I'm going to see the world," the boy replied. "Come along; we'll go together."

They travelled for some time and then met up with Seer-of-Things-in-the-Distance who asked, "Where are you going today?" "I'm going to see the world," the boy told him. "Can I come with you?" he asked. "Come on," the boy said, "Let's go."

They continued travelling until they met up with Doer-of-Things-Quickly who asked, "Hey, where are you going?" The boy told him he was going to see the world. "Can I come with you?" he asked. "Yes," the boy said.

They continued travelling for some time and saw a thief in the distance who asked, "Where are you going?" The boy told him, "I'm going to see the world." "May I follow you?" the thief asked. The boy said, "Come on, let's go."

They continued the journey until they met Potassium who asked, "Where are you going?" The boy said he was going to see the world. Potassium asked, "Can I follow you?" "Yes," the boy told her.

He collected everyone, and they travelled until they met up with Bushrat who asked them, "Where are you going?" "I'm going to see the world." "Can I follow you?" asked Bushrat. The boy said, "Let's go!"

They set off and reached the girl's town. When night fell Bushrat went into town to look for food. The boy was at the river bank listening to people talking about the girl. He did not know how he was going to meet her. Potassium asked him, "Why do you think I followed you?" She told him that she would go and tell the girl that he wanted to meet her.

After hearing the news of the boy, the girl had a servant deliver some food to them. The boy was by the river bank when it arrived. They ate the food and he filled one basket with gold coins and another with silver coins to be taken to the girl. The servant girl who had brought the food returned with the baskets.

The girl was careful not to show the senior wife what she had received. She eagerly awaited her workday so that she could cook some food for the boy. When her workday came she put some food in a bowl and underneath the bowl placed a ring. The boy was eating the food when he was surprised to find the ring. He left his food and directed all of his attention toward it.

Night fell and the boy wanted to visit the girl. The thief said, "Today I'm going to do you a favor." He took the boy to the girl and left them together. The boy and girl stared at each other for a while and spent the night talking until dawn.

At dawn the thief returned, and he and the boy left. The boy visited her regularly like this for some time until the girl became pregnant. The king announced that it was not his child, and was informed that there was a stranger staying at the river bank. "Find him!" he shouted. "Who else could be the father of my wife's child?" The king ordered his men to go kill the boy and his wife.

The thief was wandering around town when he heard this news. He went and told the boy that the next day there was going to be a fight because the king's new bride was pregnant and the people said that he was responsible. When he heard this he asked, "What can we do?" Doer-of-Things-Quickly said, "This is the day for which I followed you." Seer-of-Things-in-the-Distance said, "Here is the day for which I followed you." Dodger said, "There are no arrows or cannons which can harm me, this is my day!"

The boy said, "If I leave the girl the king will have her killed." The thief told him that he would go and steal her. The thief went to the girl and said, "Take the things that you need and let's go." She collected her things and they left. Doer-of-Things-Quickly met them on the road and hurried them to the river bank.

The king made preparations for war and was heading in their direction. Seer-of-Things-in-the-Distance warned, "They're coming!" Dodger said, "Arrows are coming! I'll defend us!" He dodged here and there and all of the arrows missed him. Everyone played their part.

The boy took his wife home and told his father, "I've returned." His father replied, "You've seen the world and even returned with a wife!" "I told you that I would only marry a famous woman," the boy said.

They were given a house to live in. His wife's pregnancy moved along and she gave birth to a boy. The other king had lost his wife.

## THE BOY AND THE OLD MAN

Once there was a girl whose husbands died soon after they married her. A man in another town heard about this girl and said that no matter what, he was going to marry her. He went and visited his malam to get some advice on how to marry the girl. The malam told him, "Use all of your cleverness to avoid galloping your horse over open places with no sand. That is the advice I give you."

The boy went to talk with the girl about marriage. After some time he sent his representatives to propose the marriage, and the wedding was arranged. That afternoon the boy went to visit the girl. He thought about what his malam had told him but later forgot the advice. When he came to an open place with no sand he galloped his horse.

As soon as he galloped over the open place with no sand he remembered what the malam had told him. When he turned and looked behind him he saw an old man following him. The boy slowed down his horse and waited for the old man. The boy asked him, "Father, where are you going?" "I'm going here," the old man replied. He was breathing heavily.

The boy dismounted and said, "Father, mount the horse." The old man refused, "No, you mount your horse." The boy said, "No!" The old man repeated, "Mount your horse," but the boy again refused. "I'll dismount and walk the horse. I feel bad that I didn't see you earlier during the journey when you began following me." He said, "If I had seen you following me and didn't stop, what kind of boy am I? Because I'm a boy and you're an old man I must offer you the horse to ride." This discussion went on for some time and finally the old man mounted the horse.

They travelled and travelled and after some time arrived in the town. The man asked, "Boy, where are you going?" He said, "I'm going to get married," and told him the story. The old man asked him, "Do you know the reason that all of the men who married her are dead?" "No," the boy replied. "I don't know what's killing them." The old man said, "Since you don't know what's killing them I'll go with you." He said, "If I go with you, you must hide me so no one sees me. When you're given a room, finished chatting and everyone is leaving, let me go into your room first. If I tell you to come in, then come in." The boy did not argue with him.

Actually, the place the boy's horse had galloped over was a town of spirits. When he rode over the town of spirits he broke the arm of a spirit's son.

When the boy arrived a mat was unrolled and people from the town came to chat with him. The young men of the town looked at him as though he was already dead. People came and talked to him about many things until it was dark. No one thought he would be alive in the morning. Night fell and he went to his room and undressed.

The old man transformed himself to look like the boy, went into the girl's room and laid down next to her. It was a black spirit who came, turned himself into a black he-goat and killed her previous husbands. He killed them by stabbing them with his horns.

The old man was lying there when the black he-goat came and saw him. The old man cut off the goat's head, put it in his sack and went and told the boy to go to his wife. The boy went to his wife and they lay there chatting until morning.

The neighbors used to come and wait by the thatch wall of the compound to hear, "He's dead!" But on that day they heard only silence. They stared at the house and waited but did not hear anything unusual. Someone looked over the wall and saw the boy coming out of the bathing area with a towel wrapped around him. After seeing that he was alive other people came and said, "We've come to greet the groom." They came and saw that he was alive and well.

After spending the wedding night the boy said that he was going home to visit his parents, and he and the old man left. When they reached the outskirts of town the old man asked the boy, "Do you know what?" "No," the boy replied. "Do you see this head of a black he-goat? If it was you sleeping in the room he would have killed you with these horns. This is what killed all of the others. Now I want you to come and see what you did to me."

They returned to the place where the boy had galloped his horse and the old man told him, "Close your eyes." The boy closed his eyes, and when he opened them saw a large town and a small boy being attended to. The old man asked, "Do you see what you did to me? This is my grandson who you trampled with the hooves of your horse. The reason that I followed you was not to go to your wife's house and help you but to kill you. However, the respect and kindness that you showed me made me do otherwise. You're a boy who knows the importance of age and who acts in a proper fashion. You and I are friends. You can come to me for anything that you need and I'll give it you."

The boy left and moved into his new house with his wife. For this reason you must respect people older than you. Hausa people say, "Showing respect to a dwarf is not useless. To live in the world you must understand it."

## THE KING'S SON WHO REFUSED TO PAY

Once there was a king's son who took goods without paying for them. Traders brought their goods to the palace and the king's son took them without paying for them. Traders would sit by the door of the palace waiting to be paid. After waiting for a long time they would leave because they knew that they would not receive their money.

One day a merchant came to town and wandered around hawking his goods. He asked, "Where can I find someone who will sell my goods for me? But I don't accept credit." He wandered through the city hawking his goods until he came to a group of people who were sitting. He greeted them and said, "Where can I find a person to sell my goods for me?" They said, "Hey merchant, if you're looking for someone to sell your goods there's someone sitting right here who will do it for you. Give them to her and she'll sell them for you. But beware, in this town there's a king's son who takes things without paying for them." The trader said, "No! It's not possible that there's someone who'll take my goods without paying for them." And he told the girl, "You, take my goods and sell them for me."

The girl went into town asking, "Where is someone who wants to buy my goods but has money in hand?" She wandered around town until she reached the courtyard of the palace. The king's son was seated in his chair with all of his courtiers seated around him. A courtier called to her, "Trader, bring the goods." She brought the goods and they bargained. The king's son bargained, agreed on a price and ordered that the goods be taken into the palace, but he did not pay for them.

The trader waited outside the door of the palace from morning until noon, but no one brought her any money. Two o'clock passed, then night fell and still no one paid her. All of the townspeople went home and locked up their houses.

The next morning she was still sitting at the door of the palace. She was tired of sitting, so she got up and went to see the merchant.

70

She told him, "Merchant, the king's son bargained for the goods but didn't pay for them. You see, I spent all day and all night there." "No, it's not possible," the merchant said. "Is there a person who can take my goods without paying for them? He doesn't exist." The girl said, "Come on, I'll take you to the palace," and she lead him to the king's son.

The merchant insulted the king's son who became angry. He was so angry that he ran and jumped into the well behind the palace. The merchant said, "No, you took my goods but didn't pay for them, and now you think you can escape? Today wherever you go I'll follow. You'll give me my money!" And he jumped into the well after him. The trader said, "Anywhere you two go I'll also follow for who will pay me for my work?" And she jumped into the well after them.

## THE MAN AND HIS CHARM

Once there was a poor man and his wife. Every day the man went to the bush to collect grass which he sold for a small sum of money. He never received more than a pittance for the grass he collected. After selling the grass he would give the money to his wife who bought food with it.

The man did this for some time and his situation did not change. His wife treated him poorly. If he was late getting out to his work she scolded him. She would say, "Now because of your lack of kindness you haven't gone to collect grass to sell, so we won't have money to buy food." The husband never said a word in response. The man was always patient and remained silent.

Time passed and one day on his way to collect grass the man came across a young snake and an older snake who were fighting. The man separated them with his stick which he always carried with him when he went to the bush. The younger snake was doing everything he could to kill the older one, so the man used his stick to carry the older snake to safety. He carried him far away and laid him down in some shade.

Then he continued on his way to collect grass. He collected and tied one bundle of grass. On his way home he passed the place where he had left the old snake and met an old man sitting there. The two men greeted each other and the man asked, "Brother, what has brought you here?" The old man replied, "I'm just resting. Where are you coming from?" The man said, "I'm on my way home from collecting grass." "What do you do for a living?" the old man asked. The man remained silent. The old man continued, "I see you're not speaking. What's the problem? I asked you a question, but you didn't answer me." The man replied, "My answer is embarrassing. In the past I did many different kinds of work which weren't profitable. But now this grass collecting which you see me doing is my occupation. I'll take this bundle of grass which is on my head and sell it for a pittance to have money to buy food. My wife

72

knows how to spend money carefully so we'll have enough food to eat. Tomorrow I'll return, and the day after tomorrow I'll return to collect grass. This has been my occupation for some time now." "This is your occupation?" "Yes," the man said.

The old man told him, "Bring me that charm that's there on the ground," and the man did as he was told. The old man made it into a charm to be worn on the arm. He gave it to the man and said, "Do you see this?" "Yes," the man replied. The old man said, "Your days of collecting grass are over. I'm telling you that you're finished with this kind of work. Take this charm and when you need something hit it on the ground. When you do this donkeys will appear which you can take to the market and sell. You may do what you want with the money. If you guard this charm your grandchildren and your great grandchildren will never be poor." The man respectfully said, "Thank you, thank you!" Then he left.

He sold his grass and gave the money to his wife and they bought food. The next morning after prayer the man refused to go and collect grass. His wife complained, "My lazy husband refuses to go to the bush. When are you going to the bush to collect grass to sell for a pittance?" The man remained silent.

When things quieted down the man got up and went behind his house, hit the ground with the charm, and large, powerful donkeys appeared. The man drove them to the market and sold them. When he returned he showed his wife the charm and she understood. After selling the donkeys he bought food, clothes and everything he needed as well as a lot of clothes for his wife. "Now I've found freedom," he said.

When she saw the charm she asked, "Husband, where did you get this?" He told her, "Well, you know that there's a reason for everything. God has witnessed my poverty and given me these things." He told her the whole story.

The man's wife had a long-time lover who she had taken because of her husband's inability to buy her things. But now she received everything she wanted from her husband. Her lover asked her, "How did your husband become so wealthy and buy so many things for your house?" She told him, "He has a charm that he wears on his arm. If he hits the ground with it donkeys appear. If he asks for 1000, then 1000 appear. If he asks for 100, then 100 appear." "We've been together for many years. Can you get this charm for me?" her lover asked. "Consider it done," she said. "If

God is willing, on Friday, the day everyone goes to the mosque to pray, come here and squat down next to the bathing area and the charm will be yours."

When her husband came home she said, "Husband?" "What?" he asked her. "Did you hear the good news?" "No, I didn't. What is it?" he asked. "The king has made an announcement," she said. "He said all men must go to the mosque this Friday to pray." Her husband said, "That's good. God is great! May he bring us to Friday."

On Friday at 12:30, when it was time to go to the mosque, she told him, "Every man's wife must bring her husband water and bathe him." Her husband agreed. She drew some water and brought it to the bathing area. The man met his wife there and undressed.

Usually the man never took the charm off of his arm, but this time he did and laid it on a rock. His wife used a lot of soap to wash him. There were so many suds that he was forced to close his eyes. Carefully she took the charm. Her lover was squatting and waiting on the other side of the bathing area. She stretched out her arm and tried to hand it to him. She could not reach him and instead dropped it on his head. Her lover became a donkey and the charm hung from one of his ears.

When the man finished bathing he put on his clothes. He looked for his charm but could not find it. His wife thought that her lover had left with the charm. The man searched the bathing area and then looked on the other side of the wall where he saw a huge donkey with the charm hanging from its ear. The man grabbed his charm and put it back on his arm. His wife saw him come from behind the bathing area with the donkey which he took to the market and sold.

Time passed and one day the woman's father came to visit. She told her father, "I have good news for you." "What is it?" he asked. "My husband has a charm which produces donkeys when he strikes the ground with it," she told him. As her father prepared to return home she gave him many gifts as well as the charm which she had secretly taken from her husband. She told him, "Take it with you. When you're finished bring it back, and we'll return it to my husband."

He took the charm and went home. When his wife saw him coming home with all of the gifts she ran out and said, "Well, hello husband! It appears you've had good fortune on your journey." He told her, "You haven't seen anything yet! I've brought a charm which produces donkeys when it strikes the ground."

He was about to show her when he inadvertently touched her arm with the charm, and she turned into a donkey. As she wandered around the compound the father took off running. When he arrived at his daughter's house she asked, "Father, is everything alright?" "Alright? Your mother has become a donkey! I was going to show her how the charm worked. When I went to hit the ground with the charm I inadvertently touched her with it, and she became a donkey."

The woman went and asked her husband for forgiveness. She told him, "You didn't know, but I borrowed your charm. When my father left I gave it to him and told him to use it and return it when he was finished. He touched my mother with it and now she's a donkey." The man told her, "There's no antidote. We can only take her to the market and sell her."

## THE IMPORTANCE OF REASON

This tale is about Reason, Wealth, Possessions, Birth and a poor man who had no children. The only thing this man owned was a large and powerful white ram. This ram was strong enough to carry a person to a faraway place.

There was a certain tree along the side of the road where Reason, Wealth, Possessions and Birth sat and chatted. It was along this road that the poor man walked on the way to his fields. He always greeted Reason, Wealth, Possessions and Birth as he passed them.

One day Wealth told the others, "If he gives me his ram I'll slaughter it and eat the meat with my family. In return I'll give him wealth." Birth said, "If he gives me his ram I'll give him a child." Possessions then said, "If he gives me his ram I'll slaughter it and eat it. In return I'll give him the finest possessions in the world." Finally, Reason said, "If he gives me his ram I'll slaughter it and eat it. In return I'll give him reason." They always talked about this.

The man passed them on his way to the fields in the morning and on his way home in the afternoon. Reason, Wealth, Possessions and Birth watched him as they sat beneath the tree chatting. The poor man, who had no sons or grandsons, passed them with his ram every day. The ram was truly the man's sole possession in life.

One day Wealth went to the man's house and said, "If you give me your ram I'll give you wealth." The man said he would think about it. Then Possessions went to visit the man and said, "If you give me your ram I'll give you possessions." The man said, "No," and Possessions left. Next, Birth went to the man and said, "If you give me your ram I'll give you a child." But again the man refused.

Lastly, Reason went and said, "If you give me your ram to slaughter I'll give you reason." "What good is reason?" asked the man. "I'll give you reason and with it you'll have a child, wealth and anything else you need or want. I can do it for you." The man agreed and gave Reason his ram. Reason said, "Do you know the tree where we sit and chat?" "Yes," the man said. Reason told him, "Go there tonight and climb the tree and hide where no one can see you. In the morning listen to our conversation. Listen closely to what everyone says. If you hear what they say you'll get anything you want!"

The man went and climbed the tree. The next morning Reason, Wealth, Possessions and Birth came and sat under the tree. They sat and waited for some time. When the man failed to come by with his ram they said, "Today our friend hasn't come. Perhaps he's ill."

Reason said, "About this man you've been pestering. I want to ask you something. Wealth, if this man gives you his ram to slaughter how will you make him wealthy?" Wealth said, "Who knows?" Then he told them that his riches were hidden in his fields in a place that no one else knew about. He explained that there was a termite mound in his fields inside of which there was a clay pot filled with gold and silver. "If a man finds this pot of gold and silver he'll be wealthy indeed!" he said. "Is that so?" asked Reason. "What about you Possessions? What will you do if he gives you his ram?" Possessions said, "If he gives me his ram what will I give him? I'll send him to a certain town to meet a man named Danga Kurda who'll help him get anything he wants." Reason asked, "Is that so? What about you Birth?" "If he gives me his ram to slaughter and eat I'll send him to a certain town to find the daughter of a certain man. If he marries this woman he'll have a child." Reason asked, "Is that so?"

Then they said, "Hey, tell us what you would do!" Reason said, "If he gives me his ram to eat I'll give him reason." They asked, "What kind of reason?" He answered, "What kind of reason? My name is Reason! If he gives me the ram I'll give him reason." They asked, "But how?" The man was sitting in the tree listening to everything that was said. He prayed for the afternoon to come so they would go home and he could come down and leave. They finished chatting and said, "I wonder if he's ill? We don't know if something is wrong or not, but he's obviously not coming today so let's go home."

After they left the man came down out of the tree and came face to face with Reason who said, "You see! What did I tell you?" The man said, "You were right!" Then he took a hoe and went to the fields to dig up the termite mound.

Meanwhile the others continued to wonder, "Where could the ram have gone? Did it die?" The man found wealth in the clay pot filled with gold and silver. Then he thought of Danga Kurda in the other town. He went to this man and told him to sell the gold for him so he could buy the things he wanted. Now the man had wealth and possessions.

After that he thought of the girl. He took off his sandals so he could run faster and set off for the girl's town. He found her, married her and she became pregnant. It is because of Reason that he was able to do all of this.

The next day Reason, Wealth, Possessions and Birth returned to sit in the shade of their tree. They said, "Now this poor man has everything. He has wealth, possessions and a child. How did this happen Reason?" Reason said, "I'll tell you. As you know my name is Reason. It was I who ate the ram and in return gave him the reason to reach his present condition. Now you're all jealous! It's because of God that he succeeded. Look at him. He has wealth, possessions and a child because I gave him reason!"

Thus, reason exceeds wealth. If someone offers to give you reason do not refuse it. Reason is wealth, not poverty. If a man says, "Come here, I'll give you something," and another says, "Come here, I'll give you reason," go to the one who will give you reason.

# TALES TOLD

## BY

## HADJIA RAHAMU

# THE HYENA, THE DOG, AND NOSE-OF-MUD

This tale is about Dog, Hyena, and Nose-of-Mud, a person whose nose is made of mud. One day Nose-of-Mud wanted to go hunting, so he went into town and asked, "Who wants to go hunting?" Cat said, "Meow!" But Nose-of-Mud told her, "You can't hunt." Dog came and said, "Woof, woof!" But Nose-of-Mud said, "Dog can't hunt either." He wanted someone who was very strong to hunt with. Along came Hyena who said, "Wawawu!" Nose-of-Mud told her, "You're a good hunter, let's go."

Hyena and Nose-of-Mud travelled deep into the bush. After some time they came across some guinea fowl. Hyena said, "Nose-of-Mud, look at those guinea fowl!" He told Hyena, "Hey, those guinea fowl belong to our town, let them pass."

They continued to travel deeper into the bush and Hyena said, "Nose-of-Mud, I'm thirsty." "Okay," he said, "We'll go to our town's large watering hole." When they arrived Nose-of-Mud said, "Hyena, drink until your stomach is completely full because after I drink there won't be any water left." Hyena drank and drank until her stomach was completely full. When Nose-of-Mud finished drinking and was replete the water was all gone.

After travelling for some time they encountered some antelopes. Hyena said, "Nose-of-Mud, look at those antelopes!" Nose-of-Mud told her, "Go and insult their mothers. When you come back go into my nose." Hyena agreed and went and shouted, "Hey antelopes, your mothers!" A small antelope asked, "Are you speaking to me?" "No," Hyena replied, "I'm speaking to the largest and strongest of you." The largest antelope asked "Me?" and Hyena said, "Yes, you!"

The antelopes chased Hyena who ran into Nose-of-Mud's nose. Nose-of-Mud caught all of the antelopes, killed them and told Hyena, "You can come out now." She came out and they picked up their kill and went home. When Hyena and Nose-of-Mud returned to town they divided up the meat and ate. Having tasted the result of the hunt Hyena decided to make a mud nose and do the same thing that Nose-of-Mud did with her.

The following week Hyena went to town and asked, "Who wants to go hunting?" Cat came and said, "Meow!" But Hyena told her, "You can't hunt." Dog said, "Woof, woof!" and Hyena told him, "You're a good hunter, let's go."

Dog and Hyena travelled for some time and then Dog said, "Hyena, look at those guinea fowl!" Hyena told him, "Those are the guinea fowl of our town, they're our little brothers."

After they travelled a long distance Dog said he was thirsty. "Okay," Hyena told him, "We'll go to that large watering hole over there and drink." When they reached the watering hole Hyena told Dog to drink until his stomach was full because after she drank there would be no water left. Dog drank and drank until his stomach was completely full and his thirst quenched. Then Hyena drank and drank, but the water showed no signs of lessening. Hyena realized that her stomach was about to burst and said, "Okay Dog, let's go."

After travelling for some time they encountered some antelopes. Dog saw the antelopes and said, "Hyena, look at the antelopes!" Hyena told him, "Go and insult their mothers. When you come back climb inside of my nose." Dog went and told the antelopes, "Your mothers!" The largest antelope asked, "Are you speaking to me?" "Yes, you!" Dog exclaimed.

The antelopes chased Dog, but when he tried to go into Hyena's nose it crumbled. They ran and Hyena said, "Dog, you take the high road and I'll take the low road, and we'll meet in town." When they met in town Dog asked, "How did this happen? From now on I'm not going to hunt with you anymore." It is for this reason that Dog and Hyena do not hunt together.

## THE MAN AND THE LIONESS

One day there was a hunter whose wife was about to give birth. The man said that if it was God's will his wife would only give birth on a lion skin. The other men said, "You're lying," and they chatted for some time about it.

The man went home and laid down until the sun came up. Then he took his bow and quiver full of arrows and went into the bush. While in the bush he searched everywhere until he came to a place where Lioness had given birth and left her children to go and find food for them. The man grabbed one of Lioness's children, slaughtered it and left her the flesh, taking only the skin home.

As he arrived home his wife went into labor. He dried the skin of Lioness's cub, and a short time later his wife gave birth on it.

When she returned Lioness looked everywhere for her missing cub. She followed the man's footprints until she saw them leading into the town. Lioness transformed herself into a beautiful divorcee and stuck an arrow in her head.

Many men asked to marry her but she said, "I don't have a bride price. I'll marry the one who can pull this arrow out of my head." A man came forward and pulled with all his might, but the arrow did not budge. A man said, "Someone is going to pull her head off. That arrow is stuck."

Many men attempted and failed. When the hunter heard the news he said, "Let me try and see what happens." The man went and easily pulled the arrow out of her head and was married to the beautiful woman.

One day she said, "I heard you're the man whose wife only gives birth on a lioness's skin." "Yes, that's me," he replied, "I'm the one." She asked him, "If Lioness sees you in the bush what will you do?" "If she tries to catch me I'll run around until I lose her," he told her. Lioness learned all of his secrets.

Time passed and one day she said, "There's something I want to do. I've seen your town, but you haven't seen mine. I want you

83

to accompany me to visit my parents. After our visit we can return here." The hunter agreed to go.

They travelled and travelled when suddenly his wife turned back into a lioness and tried to catch him. The hunter repeatedly dodged her but could not escape. He did not know what was going to happen to him. She told him, "I'm the lioness whose cub you slaughtered." He begged her to let him go, but she refused. Then the man, who was in so much trouble, was saved by the grace of God and ran away.

## THE FULBE AND THE HYENA

This tale is about a hyena and a Fulbe. One day a hyena went deep into the bush looking for something to eat. She met a Fulbe there who was carrying a water bottle and a large stick to protect himself. The Fulbe told the hyena he was going to beat her on the head with his stick, and she asked him not to do that. Then the hyena asked the Fulbe, "When are you going to die?" The Fulbe replied, "I'm going to die on Friday. You'll find me lying next to my water bottle this Friday."

The hyena went home and told her children, "There's a Fulbe who's going to die on Friday. Get ready to go and bring him here before people come to bury him."

On Friday the hyena, her husband and children found the Fulbe lying on a mat and thought that he was dead. She said, "I'm no longer afraid of his large stick." "Well my wife, what do you want us to do now?" asked her husband. She said, "We'll take his cattle and escape before any people come." He told his wife that she did not know what she was doing. "Children, what do you think we should do with him?" he asked. The children said they should kill him because when their mother said that they should take his cattle they saw his fingers move. He said, "Be quiet now. We'll tie him up and take him home and eat him. The other Fulbe will die one by one just like this one. After we have eaten all of the Fulbe we'll take their animals. Tie him to my back." The wife tied the Fulbe on her husband's back. "Now let's go home," he said.

While on Hyena's back the Fulbe opened his eyes. The children saw that the Fulbe was not dead and told their father. "This man isn't dead!" they shouted. "You're lying!" he told them. "Of course he's dead!" The Fulbe heard everything that the father said as he memorized the road they took to Hyena's house.

Early the next morning the husband went to check on the Fulbe. After the husband left, the Fulbe got up and collected his big stick and other belongings. Hyena went to say good morning to his wife. When he saw the Fulbe they stared at each other intensely for some time and Hyena began to tremble with fear. He told the Fulbe he was sorry and that he had not really intended to take his cattle.

Hyena, however, did not learn his lesson. One day he met another Fulbe and asked him the day he was going to die. The Fulbe refused to tell him.

Another day he returned to the first Fulbe's house and again asked him the day he was going to die. The Fulbe asked, "Why do you want to know the day I'm going to die?" He said, "Oh, for no special reason. It's just that if we know the day you're going to die we can announce it to the people so that a funeral can be arranged." The Fulbe told him, "Okay, I'm going to die on Friday."

On Friday Hyena told his wife and children about the Fulbe. They went to his house and found him lying in the exact same place as before. When they arrived he was lying motionless. They collected all of his things and prepared to return home. The father said, "Tie him to my back. We'll take him home and eat him today!" As they prepared to leave, the children noticed that the Fulbe was alive.

When they arrived home the Fulbe got up and said, "Hyena, you have no heart. There isn't a bone of kindness in your body. Are you trying to kill me? If so, I better kill you first." The Fulbe beat Hyena on the head with his stick. The Fulbe told him, "You'll never be able to eat me or any other Fulbe." That is the reason the Fulbe are not afraid of Hyena, and why Hyena is afraid of the Fulbe.

## GIZO, THE GIRL, AND THE TAILOR

This tale is about Gizo and his beautiful younger sister. Their mother and father died leaving Gizo to raise his younger sister, who he always treated poorly. Whenever she cooked delicious food, Gizo ate it all and left her nothing. She had to go to the neighbors to get food to eat. Also, she did not have any nice clothes because Gizo only brought her clothes that he found in the garbage heap.

One day the girl from next door came and asked her if she wanted to go to the market. She said, "If I wasn't afraid of angering Gizo I'd go with you." "Oh, don't worry about Gizo. He won't be home until this afternoon. Come on, let's go!" Gizo's sister agreed, and they went next door where she was dressed in beautiful clothes.

They went to the market and ran into Gizo. Although he remarked that she resembled his younger sister, he did not realize that it was her. He told them, "She looks like my younger sister." "Do you allow your younger sister to come to the market?" they asked. "You, the king of bossiness!" "Excuse me," Gizo said. "I was only asking." They said, "Go away and leave us alone you worthless fellow."

When Gizo arrived home in the afternoon he asked his younger sister, "Was that you I saw today in the market?" "Since you've left do you think I've had time to go to the market?" she asked. "I knew it wasn't you," he said.

While they were in the market a tailor asked Gizo's sister to marry him. She agreed but said, "You know Gizo will prevent me from keeping any nice things I receive. After you bring him the bride money don't bring me any gifts. When I come to our new house give me the things there."

That afternoon the tailor went to ask for the girl's hand in marriage, and Gizo reluctantly agreed. The bride price was paid to Gizo who did not invite anyone to the wedding.

After the wedding Gizo's sister was taken to her new home. Gizo continually visited her and took her things until one day she told her husband about the problem. Her husband told Gizo that he was not welcome in their home. If there was something that Gizo wanted from his sister he had to ask the husband who would in turn ask his wife. If she agreed she would give it to her husband and he would give it to Gizo. After this they lived in peace.

## GIZO AND THE SNAKE

This tale is about Gizo and his wife Koki. At one time Gizo and Koki had to struggle to find food to eat. During this time they blamed each other for their problems. Gizo and Koki had a snake for a neighbor, who for a long time neither of them knew was there.

One day while Koki was looking for something she saw Snake and told Gizo about him. Gizo said, "Now that we know we have a neighbor you must give him a little of everything you cook." After some time Gizo got to know Snake very well. He befriended Snake in order to take advantage of him.

One day, while they were still poor, Gizo went to his wife and said, "Our neighbor never comes out. Since he never goes out I'll ask to borrow his beautiful skin so we can leave this place. We'll leave him here and move to a new town. Who cares if he lives or dies?" Koki said, "Oh Gizo! Trust is a serious thing. If you ask in the name of God to borrow his skin he'll trust you and lend it to you. Trust is a serious thing. If you betray his trust you'll pay for it one day." "Do you know all about God? Are you the only one who knows about God? Go away and leave me alone!" Gizo shouted.

Gizo went outside and began to cry. Snake came out of his hole and asked, "Are you well neighbor? You're crying." Gizo said, "I must cry. Look at me closely and see how I am. I don't have any nice clothes because I'm a poor man. Even finding something to eat is a problem. But now I've been invited to my younger sister's wedding. How can I go dressed like this? I don't have anything to wear. How can I go? Also, I don't have anything in my house to sell in order to raise the money I need to buy new clothes. How can I go?" Snake told Gizo, "Poverty is an evil thing. If you're crying because of this, please stop." Gizo asked, "Will you lend me your beautiful skin to wear to the wedding? I'll bring it back to you. Then I'll be able to go to the wedding properly dressed." Snake replied, "Without a doubt I'll lend you my skin. All you had to do was ask for it. You must know however, that this skin is part of me.

It is my shroud, my life. If I take it off and lend it to you Gizo, I'll have difficulty finding food to eat because I'll have to stay in my hole." Gizo said, "Oh, my brother, the place I'm going to isn't far away. If I leave this afternoon I'll arrive in time for the wedding in the morning. I'll leave right after the wedding to bring your skin to you." Snake agreed and said, "In the name of God please keep this a secret."

Snake took off his skin and gave it to Gizo. He told Gizo, "With the trust of God I give you my skin. If the wind blows on me I'll die. Tomorrow when you return you must give me my skin. Now I must stay in my hole. I'll stick my head out of my hole and eat what I can catch." Gizo said, "Come on Snake! What's this talk of me betraying you? We've been neighbors for many years. Why would I betray you?" Gizo left and told his wife, "When I leave I want you to come with me. Snake can't leave his hole and he won't know if you're here or not."

Gizo betrayed Snake and moved far away. Time passed and Gizo did not return. Snake moved around as best he could. When he got a splinter he acted as if he was dying, but God was with him in his predicament. He stuck his head out of his hole and caught what little food he could. His life was difficult.

Time passed and the days soon added up to a month, and the months soon added up to a year, but Snake survived. He did not die, but he was not enjoying life either. Although he could not go out of his hole his life was still worth living.

One day Dove landed near Snake's hole and began to sing. Snake opened his mouth to speak and Dove flew away. He shouted after her, "Hey! Don't be afraid of me!" "Don't be afraid of you? You'll eat me!" she said. He told her, "If you understood my situation you wouldn't fly away from me." She said, "Snake, I've seen you climb trees and eat our eggs and kill our children. You swallow us and now that I've seen you I should stay? No way!" "For God's sake, come here and look at me," he said. "Peek inside my hole and see my predicament." She looked inside and saw his red flesh. He asked her how he could climb a tree in his condition. "How can I catch you and eat you now?" "How did this happen to you?" she asked. "Do you see that house over there?" "Yes," she said. "That is Gizo's house," he told her. "Have you heard of Gizo? He did this to me. He begged me to lend him my skin so he could go to a wedding. He told me he'd return it the following day.

Even though I've suffered I'm still alive and my days aren't over yet. If it weren't for God I'd be dead. Would you please find out where Gizo is for me? If you do, you and your children will be safe from snakes. Snakes will never bother you again." She told him, "After you get your skin back I'm the first one you'll eat!" He said, "Trust is the most important thing in the world. Because of what Gizo did to me I know the suffering caused by betrayal. Why would I betray you? Trust is the most important thing in the world. But if I do betray you, may God punish me. Even if one of my children betray your trust in the future, when you come and tell me may God take my life." She said, "Okay. But you must be patient because I don't know where he is. I'll have to search for him." He said, "God is the one who prolongs life. If God agrees that you find him, fine. If he doesn't agree then that's that."

Dove flapped her wings and took off. She looked everywhere for Gizo but did not find him or hear anyone calling his name. One day she took a long journey and landed in a tree to rest. By chance, the tree was next to Gizo's new house. Gizo was living a wonderful life in Snake's skin. The skin showed no signs of wear and appeared to be in good condition. Everywhere Gizo went people admired him. His praises were the topic of many conversations. While telling his friends about the skin he said, "The king of my city asked me where I got this skin. I didn't tell him though because I stole it from a snake who lived next door to us for many years. Who knows if he's still alive. Maybe he's still alive, but it's been a long time now. That's why I'm not afraid to boast." Dove heard everything that Gizo said.

The next day Dove landed in the tree in Gizo's compound and sang, "Who has seen Gizo in this town? Who has seen Gizo, the son of a king?" The people in Gizo's compound were busy working. Dove sang again, "Who has seen Gizo in this town? Who has seen Gizo, the son of a king?" Gizo heard the song and replied, "Dove, my little sister, come into our house and drink some water. Koki has prepared a ball of millet to make fura and added all the necessary ingredients."

Dove came down and they sat together chatting. Dove said, "I've been looking for you for many years Gizo. I even went to your old house. By the time I got there I was huffing and puffing. I did everything I could to find you but I was unsuccessful. For several years I've been going to your old house but there's nothing there."

"You didn't see anything at my house?" asked Gizo. She said, "No, I didn't see anything at your house." Gizo asked, "Since you've been going to my house do you have any news of my neighbor? I used to have a neighbor." "Who is your neighbor?" asked Dove. Gizo said, "You didn't see a termite mound with an old black snake living there?" Dove said, "What? Is there even a termite mound there let alone a snake? I've been going to your house for two years now trying to find you and I didn't see a termite mound or a snake." Dove continued visiting Gizo and she saw that Gizo enjoyed her friendship. Gizo tossed her into the air and she landed in the tree where she and her children ate.

One day Dove returned to Snake's hole. She landed in a tree to eat and began crying. She hung her head down and shook it. She said, "Snake, it's me, Dove." He struggled to open his eyes and said, "Oh, Dove, have you returned?" "Yes," she said. "What did you discover?" She said, "I met with Gizo face to face." Snake was so shocked that he took a deep breath and fainted.

Dove waited and after some time Snake woke up and asked, "You saw him with your own eyes?" "Yes," she said, "But how can I take you to his house? I can't carry you there. How could I possibly carry you to Gizo's house? Also, there's nothing I can do to trick him into coming here. I'm not cunning enough to trick him. What can I do so that you can see him?" Snake said, "Dove, I used to be heavy because of my skin, but now I am lighter. I have an idea. God will give you the strength to carry me on your back so we can fly together. We can stop to let you rest several times during the journey. If you can take me to the town where Gizo lives your work will be finished. After that you'll be free to go whereever you want."

Dove came down from the tree and Snake wrapped himself around her and rested his head on her back. She tried to fly but could not. He wrapped himself around her and mounted her a different way. He did so in such a way that he did not obstruct her wings which allowed her to fly. Dove took off. During her difficult journey she made periodic stops to rest. Snake said, "Because of God you have decided to help me. May God give you the strength to carry me there!"

They arrived safely and Gizo was unaware that Dove had brought Snake. She landed in a tree and sang, "Who has seen Gizo, the son of a king? Who has seen Gizo, the son of a king?" Gizo replied, "Dove, my little sister, come into my room and drink some water. Koki has prepared a ball of millet with all the necessary ingredients to make fura." Dove entered the room with Snake and waited for Gizo to enter. Snake unwound himself and hid between the mat and the bed. What do you think will happen?

# DAYA AND THE DODO

Once there was a woman and her husband. After some time the husband married a second wife. While the first wife became pregnant, the second wife tried everything but could not have a child. These women had to go take their own buckets to a well in order to draw water.

One day the second wife bought a slave and told him, "Go and wait inside the well. When we lower our buckets, fill mine with water and hers with sand." The slave waited by the well, and when he saw them coming in the distance descended into the well.

When they arrived at the mouth of the well the second wife told the first, "Tie the rope to your bucket." She replied, "No, you, second wife, tie your rope to the bucket." So the second wife tied her bucket to the rope, lowered it into the well and it was filled with water. After the second wife's bucket was filled with water, the first wife lowered her bucket into the well and the slave filled it with sand. They pulled it up and set it down.

The second wife lifted her bucket onto her head and prepared to leave. The first wife tried and tried but could not lift her bucket off the ground. She said, "Darn it!" The second wife told her, "Help me take mine down and I'll help you put yours on your head." "No," the first wife said. "Since your bucket is already on your head take it home and come back. Then we can divide mine and carry it home."

Every night a dodo came to this well. The first wife waited and waited until dusk. She wondered, "What will I do with this water?" Then the dodo came and joined her at the mouth of the well. He asked, "Hey you, what are you doing here?" "I've come to draw water," she replied. "You've come alone?" he asked her. She said, "No, two of us came." "Where is the other person?" "She left. As for me, my load was too heavy." The dodo asked her, "Are you a fool? Do you think there's water in your bucket?" He kicked over the bucket and sand poured out.

"You're about to give birth, so I'm going to give you a choice," the dodo told her. "Either I'm going to end your pregnancy or fill your bucket with water and allow you to leave. If you choose the second option, when your child is born he'll be my friend if he's a boy or my wife if she's a girl. Which do you choose?" She said, "It's better that my child becomes either your wife or friend. If it's a boy you'll have a friend to go to the bush with. And if it's a girl and you marry her you'll be very happy." He said, "I see that you understand." Then he filled her bucket with water and helped lift it onto her head.

When she arrived home she said, "My bucket was full of sand!" The second wife said, "Oh, I forgot! When I came home our husband gave me some work to do." As she was taking down her bucket the first wife went into labor and gave birth to a baby girl. She had a beautiful daughter and named her Daya.

Time passed and the dodo was unaware that the girl had given birth. Then one day he learned she had given birth to a daughter and named her Daya.

Daya became a young woman and was popular among the young women of the town as well as the young men. One day some girls came and said they wanted to go into the bush and collect baobab leaves with her. Her mother told them, "Daya can't go with you today." Another day the children returned and asked politely if they could go to the bush with Daya. Daya's mother said, "Okay, but don't call out her name in the bush."

They were collecting leaves when half of the girls went to another area. They came across an abundance of leaves there and yelled, "Daya! Come and collect these leaves before someone else takes them." When the dodo heard this he came quickly and asked, "Where is Daya?" The girls ran and ran until they came to a tree which they climbed. The dodo followed them and stopped next to the tree.

They waited and waited in the tree from morning until late afternoon. At that time one of the girls thought of a plan. She said, "Dodo, Dodo, leave me alone, let me come down. I'm not Daya, she's there above. She has bracelets and earrings of gold, she has two vertical scars on her cheeks, I'm not Daya." The dodo replied, "Come down, you're not Daya." The second girl also escaped this way.

Soon only Daya and her best friend were left. Daya's best friend began crying and crying, descended a bit and said, "Dodo leave me alone, let me come down. I'm not Daya, Daya is up above. She has bracelets and earrings of gold, she has two scars, Dodo let me come down." He said, "Okay, come down."

Only Daya was left and she cried. Whenever she moved, her bracelets made noise. She said, "Oh God! What am I going to do?" She did not think to take them off.

After some time Dove came and told her, "Daya take off all of these things." Daya did as she was told. She took off some of the bracelets and put them around Dove's neck. She took off the rest of them and put them around Dove's feet. Dove said, "Go and do what your friends did."

While she was crying Daya said, "Dodo, Dodo let me come down, I'm not Daya. Daya is there above, Daya has bracelets and earrings of gold. Dodo, Dodo leave me alone, let me come down." He said, "Come down, you're not Daya either." Dove told her to go down. Dove stayed in the tree and shook the bracelets and they made noise. She moved her head back and forth and Daya escaped.

When she was halfway home she met the young women and young men of the town coming to help her. They met Daya and asked her, "How did you get down?" She told them the story of how she escaped. Dove waited in the tree until Daya had made it safely home and then she flew away.

## THE GIRL WHO MARRIED A DODO

Once there was a man and a woman who lived in an isolated town. For many years they did not have any children. Time passed and one day they had a baby girl which was to be their first and only child. The girl was named Maria and she grew up to be popular among the other children. But it is not possible for everyone to like a person. The young men of the town liked Maria, but the young women did not because they were jealous of her. Her parents took good care of her, and did not allow her to play with the other girls.

The other girls plotted to take Maria to a place she was unfamiliar with and leave her there. One day a girl came to her house and they played together. The next day the girl returned and they played together again. After playing with each other for some time they became good friends.

One day the other girls decided to carry out their plot against Maria. They went to her house and asked her to come and collect wood with them. Her mother said, "No! I only have one daughter and she means everything to me. She helps me work around the house. If she leaves who is going to do the housework for me? I'm too old to do it." "Let us do the work," they said. "We'll do any work that needs to be done so we may spend half of the afternoon with Maria." She told them, "My daughter has to collect heads of millet for me." The young girls collected the heads of millet and separated the chaff. Then they pounded it and formed it into balls to make fura and tuwo. The girls did all of the work that Maria was assigned to do.

The husband told his wife, "Our daughter is not our life. If she dies or something happens to her it's God's will. We should let her go with the other girls. God is King! If she comes back it's God's will. If she doesn't come back her soul will rest in peace with God." His wife was not pleased but said, "You may go," and the girls left.

All of the girls brought along a younger brother or sister except for Maria who had no siblings. Maria said, "I'll bring our dog," and the dog followed her to collect wood.

They entered the bush and travelled a long distance until they came to a place that even the other girls were unfamiliar with. They collected wood for some time. When they finished they noticed that everyone's supplies had run out. Even their water was gone. The girls wanted to go home quickly because they were thirsty, but realized that they were lost. They walked around for a while and decided to take their wood down from their heads to rest.

After resting they put the wood back on their heads and travelled until they came upon a well. The girls did not know that this well belonged to a dodo. They peeked inside and saw water, but there was no bucket. What were they to do? There was water but no bucket.

One of the girls told another, "Go into the well and get us some water." But the girl said, "Wait, if I go in won't my little brother cry?" They told another, "Okay, you go in." But she said, "Wait, if I go in won't my little sister cry?" All of the girls refused to enter the well. Only Maria was left. They told her, "Hey Maria, you go down into the well." She said, "If I go in won't my dog cry?" "How is your dog going to cry? When you send up some water your dog will be the first to drink. Really, he won't cry."

They took Maria's head scarf and tied it around her waist. All of the girls took off their head scarves and tied them together. With all of their head scarves tied together like a rope they lowered Maria into the well and she began sending up water. All of the girls and their siblings drank some water but did not give Maria's dog any.

Then the girls began to pull Maria out of the well. They pulled her toward the top of the well and one by one took back their head scarves. When Maria was close to the top of the well, the other girls untied her head scarf from around her waist, and she fell back into the well. Maria landed on the bank of the well where there was no water and sat down. The other girls gathered their wood and started for home. They left Maria's wood, belongings and dog behind.

The dog looked among the girls but did not see Maria. He looked into the well and began crying, and Maria heard him. The dog started to go back to town, but he returned and looked into the well again. He cried some more and she heard him, but had no way to get out of the well. He went home to try and bring some people, but no one would follow him. When he returned he found a place near the well and laid down to rest. Then he dug a hole and began crying again. The dog cried and cried until he could not cry any more, and then he died with his head resting on Maria's pile of wood.

The other girls returned home. Maria's parents went from house to house asking about her. The other girls said that Maria told them she was going to collect wood from deep in the bush before returning home. Her mother told her father, "You see! They took her into the bush and lost her!" Her parents looked everywhere but failed to find her. They were patient. After some time they decided that she was dead because they could not even find her dog.

Time passed and Maria sat at the bottom of the well as her dog turned to bones. One day a dodo came to the well and spent a long time watering his animals.

Meanwhile Maria's mother cried and cried. After some time she gave birth to a baby boy and the boy grew. Whenever he went to the public meeting place the girls teased him.

One day he asked his mother, "Mother, please tell me, do I have an older brother or sister?" She told him, "You don't have an older or younger brother, but you do have an older sister. The other girls lost her in the bush and we believe that she is dead. Maybe something caught her. Who knows what happened to her?" He said, "No matter where she is I'll find her. If she's alive I'll find her, and if she's dead I'll find her grave." His parents asked, "How will you find her?" He said, "Don't worry, I'll find her."

The boy took the seed of a gourd and said, "I'm planting you in good faith. I want you to lead me to my sister. Even if she is dead and in her grave I want you to show me where she is. I plant you in good faith." The boy planted the seed and the plant began to grow.

Back at the well, the dodo threw a bucket into the well to draw some water, and Maria grabbed hold of it. When the dodo pulled on the rope he noticed it was heavier than usual. He wondered, "What's in my well? If it's something that wants to get out then it must release my bucket. When I finish I'll pull you out. If it's a jinn I'll jump in the well and we'll die together." Maria let go of the bucket, and the dodo finished watering his animals. He spent fourteen days next to the well watering them.

When he finished he did not forget what he had said. He threw the bucket into the well and said, "Whatever is in the well, get in the bucket and I'll pull you out." Maria got into the bucket, and the dodo pulled her out and looked at her. He looked at her for a long time and asked, "Are you a person or a jinn?" "A person," she replied. "What brought you here?" he asked. She told him what had happened, and to prove it she showed him her pile of wood which the wind had now blown sand over leaving only the ends of the sticks exposed. She said, "This is my wood and these are the bones of my dog. The other children led me and my dog here." He said, "I understand and I believe you." "I'm giving you two choices," he told her. "Either I'll eat you, or marry you and take you home with me. Which do you choose?" She told him, "It's better that you marry me." He asked her, "Is that what you want to do?" "Yes," she replied. The dodo put her onto the back of a camel and took her to his house. She had many luxuries at the dodo's house but no human companionship.

Time passed and one day the boy said, "Father, mother, I'm going to look for my sister. The seed I planted will show me where she is." The seed sprouted and the plant grew in the direction of the dodo's house. It climbed the outside wall of Maria's room and bore a single fruit. The boy saw the plant and followed it into the bush. He followed the plant until he arrived at the dodo's house. He saw the house, but it appeared to be empty.

After some time the dodo returned with his animals from grazing. There were cattle, camels, goats and donkeys. The boy got down on all fours and hid among the animals. He entered the compound with the goats ahead of the dodo and climbed a tree.

The dodo called his wife, "Maria!" "Yes?" she replied. "I smell the delicious aroma of a person." She said, "You smell the delicious aroma of a person? Aren't I a person?" "You're a person. But I smell the aroma of an unfamiliar person," he said. She told him, "Come in and look around." After some time he repeated that he smelled the delicious aroma of a man. She told him, "Get up and look around." The dodo looked at the gourd growing in the compound but did not see anyone because the boy was hiding in the tree.

The next morning the dodo took his animals to graze. The boy's sister came out to pound millet. While she was pounding he broke off a twig from the tree and dropped it into the mortar. She picked up the twig and thought, "This didn't fall by itself." She said, "Whatever is up in the tree must come down, be you man or jinn. The head of this house is a dodo." The boy came down and she looked at him for a while. She asked him, "How did you get in here?" and he told her. She asked him, "Who are you?" "I'm your younger brother," he said. "My younger brother? That's impossible. I don't have an older brother or a younger brother." "I was born after you," he explained. "My mother is so and so, my father is so and so." Maria hugged her brother and cried with joy for a long time. She asked, "Where can I hide you so the dodo doesn't eat you?" Maria thought of a clever plan and told her brother to climb back into the tree.

When the dodo came home he said, "I smell the delicious aroma of a person." She said, "Dodo, why are you saying that you smell the delicious aroma of a person? I'm here and I'm a person." When night came the dodo fell asleep. During the night Maria stole a camel and hid it.

The next morning she took some gold, money and food and gave it to her brother who set off for home. She told him, "I'm pregnant now. Neither you nor anyone else can come back here. Since mother and father are alive I'll come and visit them. Now you must go quickly. If you meet the dodo along the way tell him this . . . ," and her brother left.

From the well the dodo saw the boy and quickly ran toward him. The dodo asked, "Are you Maria?" The boy stopped and said, "I'm not Maria. Maria is at the dodo's house, Dodo, husband of Maria." The dodo said, "I'm the one and only husband of Maria!" and went back to the well. The boy continued on his way and the dodo came and asked him again, "Are you Maria?" The boy told him, "I'm not Maria. Maria is at home." The dodo told him, "I'm the one and only husband of Maria." The dodo went back to the well, and the boy went home.

When the boy reached home he gave his parents the gold and money and told them, "I've seen Maria." "You're lying!" they told him. He said, "My sister is alive. I'll tell you where she is. I saw her and the dodo with my own eyes. I entered the dodo's compound hidden among his goats. Maria told me that because you're alive she's coming to visit. Even though she's pregnant she's coming." The boy stayed with his parents.

101

Time passed and Maria gave birth to a son. He had the bellybutton of a dodo, but the body of a person. The girl began collecting balls of millet paste to hide her son's bellybutton.

One day after the dodo took his animals to graze, Maria loaded a camel with riches. She loaded another camel with millet balls to cover the bellybutton of her son. She left with her son on her lap holding some millet paste over his bellybutton. When they approached the dodo's well they saw the dodo who asked, "Are you Maria?" She said, "I'm not Maria. Maria is at home," and she jumped over a river.

The dodo saw her and again asked, "Are you Maria?" This time she said, "Hey dodo, take a good look! It's me!" Knowing that the dodo was unable to go into water she said, "Since I've been here I haven't been allowed to visit my family. Today I'm going home. If you think you can follow me because I have the child, here he is!" She threw the child toward him and he fell into the water. The dodo hyperventilated with anger and died. Maria's family took all of the dodo's riches. This is the reason there is a spirit of the water.

## THE TWO FRIENDS WHO MARRIED THE KING

Once there were two women who were close friends. It was the kind of friendship that one had in the old days. One day, with God's blessing, each woman gave birth to a baby girl. Since their childhood the children were friends like their mothers and did everything together. God provided them with a good life.

Time passed and when the girls were about fourteen years old they went into the bush to collect leaves from the senna plant. They were collecting the leaves when one of the girls said, "Oh!" "What is it?" the other girl said. Her friend asked, "What would happen if we returned home and the king came and asked both of us to marry him?" "We would have the usual arguments which occur between co-wives," the other girl said. Her friend told her, "No we wouldn't, that's nothing. We can stay together as friends because we're inseparable. We eat from one plate and all of our possessions are shared." The other girl said, "If God allows me to marry, I hope he gives me a son with a normal belly button." Her friend said, "If God allows me to give birth, I hope he gives me a son also, but one with a belly button of gold."

The girls returned home and after some time a messenger came to their house and announced that there was a man who wanted to marry both of them. "Who wants to marry them?" asked their parents. The messenger said, "The king." "The king?" they asked. "Yes," he told them. The mothers of the girls asked, "What are we going to do? The girls have always been together. They've always eaten together and done everything together. If we marry our daughters to the same man they'll have problems." But the girls said, "There won't be any problems." The wedding was held, and the girls were taken to the palace.

Time passed and they returned home to give birth. Both girls had sons. One of the girls gave birth to a beautiful son who looked like the king while the other gave birth to an ugly son. When the

103

girls had completed their forty days of bathing with boiling water someone said, "It's time for the girls to return to the palace."

They were escorted to the edge of town where they set out for the palace. The girl with the ugly baby asked, "May I see your baby?" The other girl agreed and they exchanged babies and tied them to their backs. The mother of the beautiful son was ashamed to ask for her baby back, and the mother of the ugly baby did not offer to give him back. She kept him until they entered the palace.

The door opened and the king came and said, "I don't like this woman or her ugly son." He told his men, "Take them away and kill them." The head of the king's men, however, refused to kill the woman and the son.

Time passed and the beautiful son played happily until he was seven years old. When he heard the hunting drums he said, "Father, I'm going hunting." "You're not old enough," the king told him. The boy decided to go anyway so he went to the stable and chose a horse to ride.

While he was riding in the bush he came across a woman sitting on the ground. When he got close to her she asked him, "Why did you come here? Why did you come to see me young hunter?" He asked her, "Where are you from?" She told him what had happened and he realized that she was his real mother.

The king's men could not find the boy and were afraid to tell the king. Then a courtier told him, "The boy is with his mother in the bush." The king did not know what to do. His courtiers explained to him that the woman in the bush was the boy's real mother. He called his head courtier and asked him, "Did you kill the woman and child as I told you?" He told the king that he had not killed them.

The king's men went and brought them from the bush. The handsome son stayed with his mother and the ugly baby was returned to his mother. The king divorced the mother of the ugly baby. He asked the other, "What do you want me to give you?" She said that she did not want anything. Now they are living together. That is why the king's head courtier is always with him when he is angry.

# THE ARAB'S DAUGHTER AND THE KING

Once there was a king and an Arab who were good friends. One day the Arab lent the king some money, and the king lent the Arab some money. The Arab had only daughters and the king had only sons. Time passed and their children grew.

One day the king sent one of his sons to collect the money owed to him by the Arab. The Arab paid the king's son the money. The king sent a message to the Arab telling him to send one of his sons to come and collect his money. When he heard this news the Arab began crying. One of his daughters asked him, "Why are you crying?" He told her, "The king to whom I lent money said he would only repay me if I sent a son to collect it." She said, "Stop crying. I'll collect your money."

Nana went to the place where her father kept his twelve horses. Among these twelve horses was one named Danda. Danda told her, "Nana, I'll take you to collect the money, but you must go and ask your father for a gown, pants, hat, many expensive clothes and some weapons."

Nana mounted Danda with all of the things he had requested. After travelling for some time they reached the king's town. Nana, disguised as a boy, went to the king's palace and greeted the people there who welcomed them. Nana announced, "Today, the Arab's son has come to collect his father's money." Nana was given a place to stay. They chatted for some time and then the king told Nana, "Tomorrow I'll give you your father's money after we have bathed." Nana said, "Okay."

She ran to Danda and said, "I'm afraid! Tomorrow I must bathe with the king." Danda reassured her, "Go ahead, you won't be shamed. Tomorrow after you wake up come and see me." When Nana arrived the next morning Danda said, "Jump over me seven times." After she finished jumping over him she became a young man.

All of the men went and bathed together. On their way back to the palace they said, "He really is a man." The king came, gave her the money and said, "Come! We must accompany the Arab's son for the first part of his return journey home." They travelled together for some time and then said their good-byes.

The Arab's daughter continued on her way while the king and his men began to return home. When the Arab's daughter saw that they were far away she yelled, "King, stop your horse! It was a young woman who came and collected the money!" The king and his men began galloping towards her on their horses. When they were close to her she threw a large object between them. The king and his men did not know what to do, and Nana rode far away from them.

A short while later they caught up to her again, so she dropped some charcoal and started a fire. The king and his men gave up the chase and returned home. Nana gave her father the money, and he thanked her very much.

When the king returned home he said, "Nana did this to me! I'll marry her and then kill her!" The king wrote a letter to the Arab saying he knew what had happened and that he wanted to marry the daughter who had deceived him. After he read the letter the Arab said, "The king may not marry my daughter." Nana said, "But father, I love him. Don't worry, he won't kill me."

The king sent all the things necessary for the wedding. The ceremony was performed and a large celebration held. After the wedding Nana was taken to the king's palace. With her belongings Nana packed ten goat-skin water bags to place in her bed at night, so if the king came to stab her he would stab the water bags instead.

One day Nana went to visit an old woman. While she was gone the king entered her room and saw the goat skin water bags under her blanket. Thinking it was her, he stabbed them. The king was surprised to see Nana the next morning because he thought he had killed her the night before.

Another day Nana put on a beautiful gown and went to visit the old woman again. As the king was passing by the old woman's house he noticed a beautiful woman in her compound, but did not recognize the woman as his wife.

The king later returned to the old woman's house and said, "I saw a beautiful woman in your compound today, and I'm in love with her." That night the king went to visit her at the old woman's house and again failed to recognize that the beautiful woman was his wife. He gave her many gifts and they slept together.

Another night he visited Nana at the old woman's house and asked her, "What do you want me to give you?" "I want you to give me your gold ring and your whip," she told him. The king gave her the things she asked for and she returned home.

Nana became pregnant and soon all the people said, "Nana is pregnant!" The king, knowing that he was not the father of Nana's child, said he would kill the man who had impregnated her. Nana told him, "Wait until I give birth to see if my son looks like you. If he doesn't you may kill me." Nana gave birth and her son grew.

One day she gave her son the gold ring and the whip she had received from the king. She sent him to the king's court to see his father. When the king saw that the child resembled him and had the gold ring and whip, he summoned Nana and asked, "How did he get these things." She told him, "You gave them to me at the old woman's house." The king said, "Yes, you're telling the truth. Now I understand what has happened."

The Arab was informed that his daughter had given birth. He went to the palace and the naming ceremony was held. The Arab was very happy. The king divorced all of his other wives and said, "Nana, you told the truth!"

## THE GIRL WHO BETRAYED HER HUSBAND

Once there were two women who were close friends. Whenever they went to the fields they went together. They went everywhere together. God allowed each of them to give birth to a child. One woman gave birth to a son, the other a daughter.

As time passed the children grew and developed a close friendship like their mothers. The two children saw how their mothers acted toward each other and did the same. This is the way it used to be in the old days. If more people followed the ways of the old days the world would be a better place. Like their mothers, these children went everywhere together as they grew up.

One day the mothers took their children to the fields and left them in the shade of a great tree under which the children wandered around and played together. After the mothers finished their work they came to pick up their children and take them home. The children, however, refused to be separated, so the girl's mother took them both home with her. The children grew up like this until they reached the age of marriage.

From the time the girl was born, however, another boy had already been chosen to be her husband. But the boy and girl said there was no one who could separate them and they were married. The previously chosen boy tried and tried to separate her from her husband, but she refused to leave him.

One day when the girl went to look for wood the other boy killed her. The husband went and searched for his wife. He came across his dead wife and saw someone digging a grave for her. He told the person to dig a grave for two people. When the man finished digging the grave the husband told the man to bury him with his wife, so the man buried them together.

After several weeks the townspeople heard their voices from the grave and came and dug them out. They returned to their house together, the girl being as beautiful as ever.

108

After some time a king heard about this girl's beauty and brought her lots of gold. He came to visit her when she was home alone, and they chatted while her husband was away. The king gave her the gold and told her that he wanted to marry her. She agreed and left her husband who had entered the grave with her.

The husband came home and searched for his wife. When he did not find her, he went into town and looked for her. He found her there and began to take her home. While they were returning home the king followed them and caught up with them. The king and the husband wrestled. They were evenly matched so the king asked the girl to help him kill her husband. She helped the king tie her husband securely with rope. Then the king picked up the husband's water bottle to take a drink. But the water in the bottle had become a large snake which killed the king. The husband ordered his wife to untie him. After she untied him he told her, "If someone asks you how I was injured don't tell them," and the girl agreed.

When they arrived home the husband's older brother asked her how her husband was injured, and she told him. The older brother became angry, took out his sword and cut her in half from head to toe.

# THE GIRL WHO BECAME A BIRD

Once there was a man who had two wives and children. One of his daughters, Maimouna, was the only child of her mother and spent a lot of time alone with her. The other children were always with their mother. In this situation one wife is always liked more than the other. It was the wife who had many children who ran the house.

Time passed and Maimouna was treated poorly by everyone in the house except for her mother. Then one day her mother became ill. She went through a period where she was ill on some days and healthy on others.

One day when she was seriously ill she told Maimouna, "My illness won't go away, and I think that I'm going to die. May God give you the patience to remain in this house. If you're able to bear it, then stay. If you find that there are times when you are unable to bear it, then go into our room until you've regained your composure. God will reward you for your efforts." Maimouna cried and said, "I'm not going anywhere. I'm going to stay in my father's house. God will take care of me." Then her mother laid down and died. From this time Maimouna had no nice clothes, sandals, dresses or good food to eat.

One day there was a festival, so she washed the only clothes she had and put them back on. The other girls lead the way to the festival and Maimouna followed behind them.

At the festival the king's son saw Maimouna and noticed her beauty. He said, "Wow! But she is too beautiful to love me." He asked his friend, "Do you see that girl dressed in tattered clothes? I want to marry her." His friend asked, "There's no one else you like besides her?" "No there isn't. I'm going to find out where she lives."

When everyone danced the girl joined them but without enthusiasm. Because her life at home was so miserable she was unable to enjoy the festival.

The king's son left the festival and called Maimouna over to him. When she arrived he asked her, "Are you from this town? Who is your father?" She told him her father's name, and he said, "You're lying. If you were his daughter you wouldn't be dressed like that. Look at how well your sisters are dressed. If he's your father why are you dressed so poorly?" "There's a reason," she said. "My mother died. Since that time things have been difficult for me because my sisters' mother doesn't like me. Even if my father wants to give me something nice she prevents him from doing so. I'm nothing in that house. When food is cooked I'm only given the scraps to eat." The king's son asked, "You're his daughter and he treats you like that?" "Yes," she said. He asked her, "Do you have a place to hide something?" "Yes, I'm living in my mother's room." He gave her some money and told her, "Go and hide this. Use it to buy food and I'll come to see you later." The girl did not tell anyone about this. She took her money home and hid it in her room.

The next morning two young men came to the house, greeted the family and said, "We're looking for the girl who was dressed in tattered clothes at the festival." Her stepmother said, "The girl from this house? Where are you?" She called for Maimouna and said, "You good for nothing! Have you stolen someone's things? Come out here, they're looking for you!" Maimouna thought to herself, "Steal? May God protect me," and she went out to see the visitors.

The king's son saw how she was treated and told her, "Yes, you're right. You are treated poorly." He told her, "I love you and want to marry you."

Maimouna had a little brother named Inni who was born just before her mother's death. She told the king's son, "This is my little brother who has just been weaned. Our mother is dead, and we're treated poorly here." The king's son said, "If God agrees your troubles will end," and they continued to discuss the situation.

Then the king's son met with Maimouna's father outside the compound and told him that he wanted to marry his daughter. The father said, "I understand, but I can't agree under these circumstances. You must ask formally by sending a marriage committee, and then I'll make my decision. But if it's her you really want I'll allow her to marry you."

Maimouna chatted some more with the king's son. After a short while he left with Inni. He bought him some clothes and sent him home again.

111

Maimouna's stepmother was angry and said, "This is foolish, worthless talk. If you're caught stealing or get pregnant I don't care! You're your father's problem." Maimouna remained silent.

The next morning the marriage committee came and announced, "We've been sent by the king's son to ask for the hand of Maimouna in marriage." The stepmother asked, "Who? You must mean one of my daughters." They said, "No, it's the other girl we've been sent to ask for." The woman named her three daughters, but the men said, "No, it's none of them. We've come for the other girl." The stepmother said, "You've come to ask for her hand in marriage while her three elder sisters have yet to marry?" The men explained, "The king's son said it was Maimouna he wanted." The stepmother asked, "This stupid, messy girl?" "Yes," the men answered, "It's her we were sent for. Maimouna's father said that he would grant the king's son's request. Let's not waste any time," the men said. "Here are all the things necessary for the marriage. Tell Maimouna to prepare for the wedding." Shortly thereafter Maimouna was married and taken to the king's son's house.

One day her stepmother saw the hairdresser on her way to braid Maimouna's hair. She told the hairdresser that she would go and braid her stepdaughter's hair.

The stepmother visited a malam and told him that she wanted a special charm. She took the charm with her to braid her step-daughter's hair. The stepmother thought, "This girl lives in the palace while my daughters remain unmarried. She deserves to be chased into the bush." While braiding Maimouna's hair she braided the charm into it.

After her hair was braided Maimouna turned into a bird and flew into the bush. The town was in an upheaval. The king's son, the king and everyone else searched for her. Even her stepmother searched for her. They searched and searched but could not find her.

Her younger brother woke up every morning and went walking in the bush to watch birds. One day Inni went out at dawn to a large tree where all the birds slept. A bird took off and flew away, and he watched it.

When the sun had just begun to rise he heard a bird say, "Stepmother, Stepmother." Inni looked into the tree and realized that it was his sister. When he recognized that the bird was his sister he said, "Hello in your trouble Maimouna. Hello in your trouble, do you hear me?" When she heard her brother's voice she flew to another tree, but he followed her and repeated, "Hello in your trouble Maimouna. Hello in your trouble, do you hear me?" She told him, "Go home and find some food to eat Inni, go home and find some fura to drink, go home and find some koko to drink." He replied, "Even if I go home sister they won't give me anything. They won't even give me my own clothes to wear, not even a pair of pants. I'm going to where the sun sets Maimouna."

After he found his sister Inni stayed with her. He did not look for food nor did he return home. He wandered around with her and followed her until the afternoon. He was watching her when she took off and flew back to the other tree and went to sleep.

Inni spent three days in the bush with his sister and then went and told the king's son that he had found Maimouna. The king's son said, "Stop lying." "I swear I saw her," he told him. "She's in a large tree where all the birds sleep. I went there and one of the birds got up and spoke. She flapped her wings and said, 'Stepmother.' I spoke to her and she answered me." "What did you do?" asked the king's son. "I stayed with her for a while, and then I came to tell you." Inni said, "Come with me and hide so she doesn't see you, and I'll talk with her."

When Maimouna realized that her brother visited her regularly she stayed in the same tree. When they arrived at the tree the king's son hid nearby. Several birds made noise and flew away. Then Maimouna stepped forward and said, "Stepmother, stepmother." The boy asked, "Did you hear that? But we can't climb the tree because she won't let us catch her that easily."

Inni said, "Hello in your trouble Maimouna, do you hear me?" She came out of the little house that she had made and said, "Go home Inni and find some food to eat, find some fura to drink. Go home Inni and find some koko to drink." He replied, "Even if I go they won't give me anything. They won't even give me my own clothes to wear. They won't even give me a pair of pants. I'm going to where the sun sets, do you hear me?" She moved around in the tree and he kept his eye on her. They spent the afternoon in the bush without eating or drinking anything.

When they returned home the king's son told his father that he knew where his wife was. "Where did you see your wife?" asked the king. He said, "She's a bird," and explained the story of how her younger brother found her. "But how are we going to catch the bird?" asked the king. They found someone with a slingshot and decided to shoot her in a place that would not seriously injure her. "After she is stunned and falls to the ground we can catch her. If we don't do this we won't be able to catch her," said the king's son.

They gathered all the young men who could shoot a slingshot, chose the most accurate shooter amongst them, and headed off into the bush. The boy who was going to shoot hid alongside of the king's son and the king's men.

Inni sang to her like he had before. A bird appeared and flew away. Another bird came, flew away and someone yelled, "That's her!" Another said "No, it isn't." Then Maimouna came out and said, "Stepmother." The boy said, "That's her!" When she heard her brother speak she came out further onto the branch. The shooter readied his slingshot and let go a shot that hit her on the wing. She fell towards the ground. When they caught her they noticed a lump on the crown of her head. They examined the bump more closely and discovered that it was a charm. When they took the charm out of her hair she turned back into a person. She was thin. Someone asked, "What are we going to do with this girl?" Another said, "Take her home and take care of her. When she gets better we'll have another wedding."

She was taken to the king's palace and attended to by the king's wife. After some time Maimouna recovered and looked even more beautiful than before. The king's son was happy with the situation.

An announcement was made in the town. The people of Maimouna's old house and neighborhood were forbidden to pass by the palace. If one of them was caught doing so they would be taken away and beaten. The only person allowed to come to the palace was her younger brother who lived with her. They are now living like this at the king's palace.

# THE MAN WHO BECAME KING

Once there was a man who lived in total poverty. He always said that if it was God's will he would become wealthy. One day a friend of his told him, "If you want to become king that isn't a problem. But you must be resourceful."

One day the man came home and wondered, "What can I do to become wealthy? What can I do to become king?" He always told his mother that he would one day be king, but that he would have to deceive people to do it.

One morning he asked his mother for two pieces of gold. She gave them to him and he set out for the king's palace on his horse. When he arrived there he asked if the king was in. The king's men told him that he was. "I want to see him," said the man.

The king and his courtiers came from inside the palace. When he appeared, the people greeted him. The man said, "Long live the king! I've come with a horse that defecates gold." The king was surprised and asked the man, "Golden feces?" "Yes," the man told him. "You're lying!" said the king. "Let's go," the man said, "I'll show you." The king said, "Okay, let's go see the horse."

They went to the horse. The man hit the horse and it defecated. He picked up a piece of the feces, broke it open and took out a piece of gold. The king took the other piece of feces, opened it and also found gold. He asked the man, "Will you sell me this horse?" "Of course I'll sell it to you your highness." "I'll give you half of my wealth in exchange for it," the king said. "Do you agree?" The man agreed, and the king gave him half of his wealth. The man took his new-found riches and went home.

The king ordered many storage houses built to hold all of his gold. Many people came to assist with the building of the storage houses and collection of the gold. They worked all day but found no gold in the horse's feces. The angry king summoned the man.

When they heard the news his mother tearfully told them, "We must go and see the king." The king decided to punish the man, and his mother cried. The man told her, "Don't give me a hard time!" He took a knife and stabbed his mother in the stomach and blood poured everywhere. She pretended to be dead. The man said, "She isn't dead! Bring me a calabash bowl full of water!" He put his knife in the water and his mother woke up.

The king said he wanted to buy the man's knife. He had forgotten about the previous trick the man had played on him. The king went into the palace with the knife and water. He chose his favorite wife, stabbed her in the stomach, and she died. The king told them, "Don't worry!" He took the calabash bowl and put his knife in the water. He poured the water on his wife, but she did not get up. The king was angry and ordered his men to go and bring the man.

When he arrived the king told him, "I'm not listening to your lies anymore." He put the man in a leather sack, tied it shut and took him deep into the bush. The man was left alone there tied in the leather sack.

After some time he heard someone coming. It was a man and his donkey on their way to town to sell his goods. The man inside the sack began screaming, "I don't want to be king now!" The man with the donkey said that he wanted to be king and untied the bag. When he got into the bag the man tied it shut and threw it into the river.

He returned to the king's palace and told the king that he had just come from Paradise. He said, "Paradise is wonderful! There's a lot of food!" Believing that the man had died, gone to Paradise and returned, the king ordered his men to put him in a leather sack. They took him into the bush and threw him into the river so he could go to Paradise. The man called the king's men and told them that the king was never coming back. "Now I am king!" he told them.

## THE BOY AND THE SPIRIT

Once there was a boastful king's son who thought himself better than everyone else in the town. If he cleared his throat people came to see what he wanted.

In another town there was a king's daughter who was very haughty. She refused everyone who came to marry her whether they were wealthy or poor. There was no one acceptable to her. Her father was upset about this and did not know what to do with her.

One day the king's son told his father that he was going to see the world. His father told him, "Go and look at all of my horses and choose one." The boy went and chose his father's favorite horse. The horse he chose was one his father had bought from a spirit. It was not the horse of a person. This horse had ridden from the easternmost corners of the world to the westernmost, from the westernmost to the northernmost and from the northernmost to the southernmost.

He showed his father the horse that he chose and his father asked, "This horse?" "Yes," the boy replied. "Are you sure you want this horse?" "Yes," he repeated. His father warned him, "You've taken on a burden, but I'll tell you something important about this horse. Don't beat him, whatever you do don't beat him with a whip. This horse will take you anywhere that you want to go in the blink of an eye, but don't beat him. Whatever you do, don't mistreat him!" The boy said, "Okay."

The boy began his journey. At the outset he rode his horse slowly, but when he reached the outskirts of town he had a feeling of elation and hit the horse with the whip. The horse began galloping quickly and carried the boy to a place where large, black ants lived and left him there.

A spirit came out, grabbed the boy and broke one of his arms and one of his legs. She forcibly took away his nice clothes and give him tattered ones instead. Then the spirit gave him a small calabash bowl, a small drinking gourd, an old hat and told him, "If you

117

continue travelling in that direction you'll come to a town. In this town you'll stop and stay at the king's palace. If you have a problem there, come back here and pour the water from this drinking gourd into this hole and wait. If God agrees I'll appear." After that she disappeared, leaving him alone.

The boy continued on his way. When he arrived in the town he greeted the people and went to the king's palace. "Where are you from?" asked the king. "That's not important," he replied. "I've come to ask for your daughter's hand in marriage." The king summoned his daughter. When she arrived he asked her, "Do you want to marry this man?" She looked at him and said, "Yes, I like him." Shortly thereafter they were married.

The girl's house had several stories. After the wedding the boy was taken and given a place to stay on one of the floors where there was running water and a bathroom. The next morning the king had food and many things sent to them. The girl, however, kept everything for herself and cooked only chaff and potassium for him. The food was served to him in a broken bowl.

One day he went and told the spirit about his problem. "Be patient," she told him. Time passed and the boy was patient. After some time he returned and told the spirit about the poor treatment he was receiving. The spirit told him to bring the bowl and chaff that he was given to eat as proof. The boy brought the things and showed them to her.

One day the girl was out for a walk and decided to go and visit the animals in the palace at the place where they were tethered. While she was on her way someone came and told her that all of her cattle had been raided. "Go and rescue them!" she shouted.

Faced with this problem the husband again went to consult the spirit who told him, "If you go to help her and all the young men of the town are there don't worry, only you can recapture the cattle."

The boy went after the raiders, but the others were afraid to go with him. The cattle could be seen in the distance. The other men also saw them but were afraid to go with him. The boy approached the cattle from the east. The others said, "He's a prophet!" Someone else said, "He's not a prophet, he's a man." Another said, "We've never seen this type of man!"

The spirit came and said, "Greetings young men of the town. What are you doing here?" "We want to rescue the king's daughter's cattle which have been raided," they answered.  And the spirit left.

The boy came and told them, "I can bring the cattle to you, but each of you must give me one of your little fingers and little toes." They agreed.  The boy gave them to the spirit, and in return she gave him riches.  The cattle were rescued and returned to the king's daughter.  Now the man and the king's daughter live together.

## THE MAN WHO MARRIED A DONKEY

Once there was a woman who wanted to have a child. Although she and her husband were wealthy they had no children. The woman spent a lot of time in her room crying. She said, "If I die all of our wealth will be useless because we have no children to inherit it." She prayed, "God, please give me a child."

Time passed and the woman became pregnant. One day she went into labor and gave birth to a baby donkey. In spite of this she was very happy and bought a slave for her child. This child was a troublemaker. If a pot of food was put on the fire to cook, she would break it. If they filled a pot with water, she kicked it over. When food was brought to her she dumped it on the ground.

One day the mother told the slave, "In the morning take some food and drive my daughter into the bush and let her graze. In the afternoon bring her back to the house." The slave girl took the donkey and drove her into the bush to a place where there was a large watering hole and a large tree. They spent the afternoon there.

One day the donkey asked the slave girl, "Do you know what I want?" "No," she replied. The donkey said, "Before we leave home tomorrow I want you to steal me some soap, a scrub brush, some flowers, kola nuts, antimony and body oil." The slave girl said, "Okay," because she was afraid to disobey the donkey.

When they returned home the slave girl stole everything the donkey asked her for. The donkey took the things and hid them. When the time came to leave in the morning she collected the things. They arrived at the large tree and the donkey looked around in all directions to see if anyone was watching them. When she saw that there was no one around she took off her skin, went to the bank of the watering hole and bathed.

When the girl bent down to wash herself Sun howled, "Kurururu." Moon said, "Be careful sun." Water asked, "Should I dry up?" The girl said, "If you dry up, what will I wash myself with?" Earth asked, "Should I sink?" The girl said, "If you sink

120

what will I stand on?" The girl entered the watering hole and bathed but kept her donkey skin close by her. After she bathed she ate her flowers and kola nuts. They spent their afternoon there and ate their food.

The king's son was in a nearby tree watching the girl. He wanted to come down, but he did not want her to see him. Late in the afternoon she put her donkey skin on and left.

The king's son took off running. When he arrived home he said, "Mother, mother, I want to marry the donkey. Father, I want to marry the donkey." They said that he should marry the daughter of another king, but he refused. His mother and father agreed to marry him to the donkey. The king's son's family went and asked for the girl's hand in marriage, and the donkey's family agreed. Everything was done as if she was a person. The donkey was prepared for marriage and the wedding was held. After the wedding she was taken to the king's son's house and given a room.

In the morning the donkey tapped her slave to wake her up. She told her to put water in the bathing area for her. The donkey went into the bathing area, took her off her skin and bathed. The king's son did not know where to find medicine to turn her back into a person. He said, "This woman isn't a donkey. There's no one in this land as beautiful as her." He told a friend, "She's only wearing a donkey skin. I've seen her take it off to bathe." His friend told him, "Find some Indian hemp, the shrub with white sap and some pepper, and pound them together. You must conspire with her slave and have her spread this mixture on the inside of the donkey skin. After that she won't put the skin on again."

The king's son called the slave girl and asked her, "Do you know where my wife is? I have medicine that will separate her from her donkey skin. When she gets undressed to bathe rub this medicine on the inside of her donkey skin." The slave girl agreed.

At dawn the girl got up to bathe. She washed while it was still dark so no one would see her. She woke up her slave girl who brought her water. Then she began bathing herself. While she was bathing the servant girl rubbed the medicine into her donkey skin. After her bath she took the donkey skin and put it on, but it itched a lot because of the pepper so she took it off.

Her beauty illuminated the entire neighborhood. The muezzin got up at dawn to perform the call to prayer. He looked at the door of the king's palace, saw the great light and went back inside. A while later the leader of the prayers thought, "The muezzin is late with the call to prayer, let me see what the problem is." When he went out he saw the light and went back inside.

The king announced that everyone must gather in his court. The girl put on her best clothes and told her slave to lay a carpet of kilishi from the center of her room to the king's court. They went to the king's court. When the king saw them coming in the distance he put his hand in a calabash bowl of sweet millet balls. The girl was so beautiful that he stood with his mouth open so that flies went in and out. He stared at the girl like this until his drool filled the calabash bowl. The girl bowed and said, "Father give me a gift so I may leave, I'm tired of bowing." He formed a ball of sweet millet and gave it to her. He now understood where the light was coming from.

A day went by. The second day the king said, "This is war!" The king's son knew that he was going to have to fight his father in order to keep her.

The girl took her comb and braided a date pit into the king's son's hair, and he went to fight. They spent many days in the bush discussing the problem but did not fight.

After some time they became thirsty. They came to a well, but there was no bucket. "Now what are we going to do?" Someone said, "If we tie all of our turbans together one person can be lowered into the well to get water." The king said that his son would go into the well and get everyone water to drink. The king's son's turban was tied around his waist and everyone else's tied end to end to form a rope. The king's son was lowered into the well, and he gave them water to drink.

After some time everyone took back their turbans. When only the king's son's turban remained the king shouted, "Let him go," and his son fell back into the well. He did not land in the water however, he landed on the bank of the well standing up. The king ordered that the well be filled with stones. After they left the date pit that was braided into his hair began to grow up out of his head, and he was able to climb out.

He sat down and saw the slave girl on her way home from milking the animals. "Hey, girl," he said, "In the name of God give me some of that milk to drink." She told him, "No, this milk's for your wife. Why would I give it to you?" The man got up and went home to his wife. Now they live together.

## THE BOY AND THE WITCH

Once there was a woman who only gave birth to girls. As her four daughters reached the age of puberty she became pregnant again, this time with a foolish boy.

Her daughters heard about a certain hairdresser and one of the girls said, "We're going to go to the hairdresser." Their mother asked them, "Do you know this hairdresser?" "No," they replied. "But we've heard that she's very good." Their mother said, "Well, there are many hairdressers in town." But they insisted on going to the one that they had heard about.

From inside his pregnant mother the boy said, "Wait, we'll go together." After hearing the unborn child speak the mother sat down. The daughters looked at her and asked, "Where did that voice come from?" "Here I am inside of our mother," the boy said. They asked their mother, "What's going on?" She told them, "My unborn child can talk!" The boy told his sisters, "It's I who spoke, do you think your mother would lie? We'll leave together, I'm Dan Kutungaya!"

Soon after this the woman gave birth to her son who was born wearing a shirt, pants and a hat. He got up to follow his sisters and they told him, "You can't follow us." "I'm going to follow you," he persisted. They beat him and forced him to stop. They travelled a long way, but he continued to follow them. They told him, "If you're going to misbehave so will we," and they killed him.

He got up again, became a fly and attached himself to his oldest sister. They travelled for a long time before they reached the hairdresser's town. The hairdresser they were going to see was actually a witch who killed people, cooked them and ate them. Coincidentally, this witch had four sons and her youngest child was a daughter, the opposite of the sisters' mother.

When the sisters arrived in the town their little brother was with them and he declared, "I've followed you." The second oldest

123

sister said that she was going to send him home, but the oldest sister said, "Leave him alone, let him be."

The witch greeted them and the boy watched her closely, examining her every move. The witch told them, "You must wait until tomorrow for me to do your hair because it's getting dark now." She gave them some household chores to do and went into the bush.

The boy went into the room where they were going to sleep. With a lot of patience and hard work he dug a long tunnel from the room to their house. Then he went back outside, sat down and began playing with the witch's youngest child.

When it was dusk the witch gave them some blankets. She gave her children black blankets, the other children white blankets, and they all went to sleep. The four sisters each had a scarf around their neck when they fell asleep. Their brother got up and carefully removed the scarves from his sisters' necks and placed them around the witch's sons' necks. Then he took the black blankets and put them on his sisters and put the white ones over the witch's sons and went to bed.

When the witch came sharpening her knife he was asleep. She felt for the scarves and killed the children wearing them. Thinking that they were the sisters, she killed all four of her sons and left.

After she left the brother woke his sisters and said, "Get up! Do you see what happened? She wanted to cut off your heads! Where are your scarves?" They felt their necks and saw that there were no scarves. "There they are," he told them. "She killed her own children because she thought they were you!" The sisters went into the tunnel and escaped.

That night the witch prepared the dead children for cooking. The next morning the sun came up, but the witch did not see her children. "Maybe they haven't gotten up yet," she thought. She finished cooking the meat and waited for them to come and eat. She shouted, "Get up! What kind of sleep is this?" She went to check on them and found only her youngest child and the boy. The witch asked, "Where are the rest?" They said, "We haven't seen them."

The witch went into the room and saw nothing but blood and blankets and asked the boy, "Where are your sisters?" "My sisters?" he replied. "Shouldn't I be asking you that question?" The witch asked, "What do you think you're doing?" "Don't you know my power?" the boy asked her. She said, "No, I don't." He told her, "Today you'll witness my power. It was your children that you killed you useless, stupid witch. My name is Dan Kutungaya!" "You did this to me?" she asked. "Yes," he told her. "All of the evil things that you do will end with you. If you eat that meat it's your children that you'll be eating. The others that you intended to kill have gone home." She tried to catch him but he took off running and jumped into the tunnel and escaped.

The witch sat down and began crying. She left the meat and it began to spoil until finally she ate her children. Only her youngest child was left. The witch took her daughter everywhere with her. The witch thought, "What can I do to get even with that boy?" She said, "I must take revenge. I'll turn myself into a mare and go into town. If God wills it the boy will mount me. If he doesn't mount me, and someone else does I know what I'll do to him."

She took to the road and went into town. The boy was playing with some children. When he saw the mare he said, "Wait, look at that mare wandering around over there. I'm going to ride her." He mounted the horse and began beating her with a whip. She said, "Dan Kutangaya, it's me!" "That's why I'm beating you," he said. He beat her with the whip and she ran here and there until by God's grace she found the road leading into the bush.

She rode to her house, threw him into a hole and turned back into a person. She told her daughter, "Come and stay here. I'm going to get some wood so we can cook this stupid boy."

After she left the girl peeked into the hole. The boy took a handful of sand and began eating it as if it was something delicious. The girl said, "Oh, Dan Kutangaya give me some!" "I've been put in a storage bin of aya," he told her. "You must come into the hole and give me your clothes if you want me to give you some." She went into the hole, took off her clothes and gave them to him.

When the witch returned he said, "Hello, mother." The witch threw the wood into the hole, started a fire and cooked her daughter. The witch took out the meat and ate her child. The boy had tricked her again. Now you have heard how Dan Kutangaya tricked and killed them all.

## ALWAYS-ON-ONE'S-BACK

Once there was a woman and her husband. He was the first man she married, and thanks to God they were wealthy. God, however, did not give them any children, so the woman went to see a malam and a boka. She tried everything because she desperately wanted to have a child.

One day she said, "God, please give me a child, even if it's a child who always wants to be tied to my back. God, please give me a child, allow me to give birth. If I die all my wealth will be lost without an heir. My husband hasn't married another wife even though I haven't had a child." Then she travelled into the bush and her prayers were answered. A spirit heard her request and entered her body.

A month passed, two months passed, three months passed. Some people said, "She's pregnant." But other women said, "No she isn't." They argued, "Yes, she's pregnant." The woman was indeed pregnant, and as her pregnancy moved along her belly grew bigger.

When the time came she gave birth to a son and was happy. People came to their house and the naming ceremony was held. It was now permissible for him to be tied to his mother's back. The woman preferred to spend most of her time in her room alone with her son.

One day the woman unknowingly made the mistake of tying her son to her back. After she finished her work she wanted to put him down and said, "I guess I'll put him down now." She went to untie him and he said, "Ihi!" "What?" she asked. He said, "I'm Always-On-One's-Back." Whenever he was hungry he said, "Ihi! Milk!" When he said this she untied him and gave him some milk. After she gave him some milk he said, "Ihi! I'm Always-On-One's-Back." He was always on her back. She even had to go to the bathroom and sleep with him tied to her back.

The woman began to become thin and lose her beauty, but her son refused to leave her back. She did not know what to do so she went to see a malam and a boka. She went everywhere looking for help. She searched here and there for medicine which would get her son off her back, but everything failed.

After some time she visited a malam who said, "I'm going to tell you what to do to get your son off of your back. Find a large he-goat and take your son into the bush. When you're in the bush say, 'Always-On-One's-Back?' And he'll ask, 'Yes?' Tell him, 'Sit on the back of this he-goat while I go to collect some wood. When I finish I'll return and tie you to my back.'" Because God had given this woman wealth, and she could afford to buy a he-goat, she agreed to do what the malam told her.

The woman bought a he-goat, went to a place deep in the bush and said, "Always-On-One's-Back, come and sit on the back of this he-goat so I can go and collect firewood. When I finish I'll return and we can go home together." "Okay," he replied. She untied him from her back, put him on the back of the he-goat and left for home. She thought, "I've had good fortune for God has rid me of my son."

The boy waited on the back of the he-goat until dark. Hyena was out looking for food and not having much luck when she came across Always-On-One's-Back on the he-goat. Hyena said, "A boy and a he-goat? Hey boy, will you give me your he-goat to eat?" "No!" said Always-On-One's-Back. Hyena said, "Please give me your he-goat to eat." He told her, "I refuse. It's the goat whose back I'm always on." Hyena said, "Come and sit on my back. It's much more comfortable. Give me your he-goat to eat and I'll tie you to my back."

The boy got down off of the he-goat, went and drank some water and climbed on Hyena's back. Hyena said, "Hey, you, stupid boy! Get down off my back, I'm not your he-goat." He said, "No! I'm Always-On-One's-Back!" Hyena told him, "No, you're not!" and tried to kick him off. The boy refused to move so Hyena tried everything to get him off her back. Hyena did not know what to do with the boy. After some time Hyena grew thin and was in poor health. The boy was wearing her down.

One day Hyena dropped to the ground and rolled over and over saying, "Bastard, I'll kill you!" But the boy remained on her back. She said, "So that's the way you want it," and Hyena went into a thorn bush and rolled around. But Always-On-One's-Back

127

remained on her back, and Hyena again did not know what to do. Her poor health continued.

She left and was blown around by the wind until she met up with Jackal who asked, "King of the bush, how did you get so sick? And what is that boy doing on your back?" Hyena explained, "I got this useless boy when I ate his he-goat. He wants to kill me." "Go away with your problem," Jackal told her. Hyena pleaded, "In the name of God my brother, please get this boy off my back." "Impossible," Jackal replied. "You ate the meat. Did you offer me any?" Hyena said, "If I get some tomorrow I'll give it to you." "Go away with your problem!" Jackal told her.

After travelling for some time Jackal changed his mind and decided to return. He whispered into Hyena's ear, "You must act as if you're dead and not move. If he thinks that you're dead he'll leave." Hyena agreed that this was the best solution.

She fell to the ground and opened her mouth allowing flies to go in and out. She laid down and remained motionless. "Are you dead?" the boy asked. Then he got off Hyena's back and left. When Hyena heard him leave she shook herself a final time to make sure that he was not there. Hyena thought, "Jackal certainly is kind. Thanks to his help I feel better now." Then she took off running towards her home.

When she arrived home she began playing the goge. She said, "My children, my children, come here! I'm going to play music for you." Hyena began playing and sang, "Son of a dog, bastard, stupid boy! I'm rid of him, Always-On-One's-Back, with stupid eyes! Always-On-One's-Back, I'm rid of him, the fool!"

After Hyena's youngest daughter heard this she went wandering in the bush and sang the song. Always-On-One's-Back heard her but did not say anything. He disguised himself as a beggar boy and went to Hyena's home saying, "Where are my alms?" Hyena said, "Beggar boy, come here." He came in and Hyena told him, "I want to play you a beautiful song, but I'm afraid of you because you have the eyes of Always-On-One's-Back." "Who is Always-On-One's-Back?" he asked. "Is he a man or a spirit?" Hyena said, "He's a boy. A stupid, impolite boy. If you didn't look so much like him I'd sing the song for you." "I'm not him," the boy told her. So Hyena sang for the boy, "I'm rid of him, the fool, son of a dog. Fool, the one with red eyes, Always-On-One's-Back. Son of a dog, bastard, fool!" The boy asked, "Are you singing about me?

Is it me you're singing about?" Hyena replied, "Honestly, I was singing Always-On-One's-Back, the well-fed and well-rested one." Always-On-One's-Back grabbed Hyena and beat her. She lost control of her bladder and bowels. "I apologize princely one!" shouted Hyena as she ran away. Always-On-One's-Back also left.

The woman who wanted a child said she would accept whatever God gave her, and as a result her son almost killed her. Whatever God gives you, accept it. If God does not give you something do not beg him for it. Do not pray for just anything.

## THE BOY AND HIS FATHER

Once there was a boy and his father who were poor, mean-spirited people. One day the father chose a fertile piece of land deep in the bush and took his son there. He did not want to continue living like he was. The father told his son that they had to go and prepare the field for planting. The father and his son spent many days weeding the field, and when they finished they burned the weeds.

The father looked north, south, east and west and said, "If God brings rain I'll have plenty of food from this field that I've weeded. I'll also buy a horse which I'll ride very fast to make a tour of this place. If I sell the harvest from the field I'll be able to buy a horse." His son said, "Father, if you buy a horse I'm going to ride it." The father leapt up, axe in hand and said, "Bastard, I'll buy the horse and you'll ride it? You'll probably kill it." The father approached the boy with the axe and struck his son until he lost his senses and stopped breathing. The man took his axe, put it over his shoulder and left, thinking that his son was dead.

The boy was lying there in the bush when, thanks to God the protector, a man came by. It was the time of day when one relaxes, and a wealthy man happened to be out riding his tall, well-adorned, slow walking camel.

The man saw some birds in the shade of a tree and wondered, "What's that over there?" He decided to go and see and came upon the boy. The camel began to descend but did not move quickly enough so the man jumped off. He ran over to the boy and held him. He took a kettle and heated some water which he used to wipe the blood off of the boy. He unrolled a carpet and put him on top of it so he would be more comfortable. He examined the boy to determine his condition and saw that he was alive and breathing. Realizing that he was still alive the man thought that maybe he was thirsty and hungry. He opened the boy's mouth and poured in some water, but the boy did not move.

After some time he noticed the boy licking his lips. The man thought, "He's still alive." The man, who had only intended to go out for some fresh air, spent a week attending to the injured boy. He began to get better, and the man asked, "Boy, how did you end up way out here in the bush in this condition?" He raised his head, looked at the man and said, "This isn't far in the bush. This is the field that my father and I worked together. He was waiting for God to bring the rain so we could plant. After we harvested the millet he was going to sell it and use the money to buy a horse. Then I said, 'Father if you buy a horse I'm going to ride it.' It was because I said that I would ride his horse, which he hadn't even bought, because God hadn't yet brought the rains, that this happened to me." "Your birth father did this to you?" the man asked. "Yes," the boy replied. The man said, "Tell me the name of your town so I can take you to your father and he'll know that you haven't died." "No," the boy told him. "I'm not returning to him. My head is unclear and I've forgotten where I'm from." The man said, "Okay son, between God and I, between the Prophet and I, I'll tell you that I'm a wealthy man. People in the north, south, east and west know me because of my wealth, but I have no children. I'll take you to my home and tell them that you're my son. I'll treat you as my own. Don't hesitate to ask me for things. If it's wealth that you want you won't have to do anything to get it. You'll be like my own child. If God decides to take my life, all of this wealth will be yours. You trust me and I'll trust you." The boy agreed, and the man put him on the back of his camel and set off for his home.

When he arrived home his wife said, "You've been gone a long time." "Yes," he replied. "I've been thinking about home. You know that since we've been married we haven't had any children so I decided to bring my son from a previous marriage. I passed by to pick him up and bring him here. You see I left him in his village until he grew up a bit."

One day the man told him, "Now you're old enough to marry. Look at the young women and choose one, I'll take care of the wedding for you." "Father, the girl I've heard about and want to marry is the daughter of a king. She has refused everyone who has asked to marry her. My friends have told me about her, and it's her I want to marry. I would like you to prepare a wedding for us. I need some expensive perfume, incense, a sack of kola nuts and some

131

slaves, and then I'll go and ask her to marry me." The man said, "I'll give you everything you've asked for."

When he reached the girl's town he dismounted his horse at an old woman's house. She greeted him and asked, "Where are you from?" The boy told her, "That's not important. I need a place to stay. May I stay here?" "Yes," the old woman said.

The old woman went and told the king's daughter, "I have good news for you." The king's daughter asked, "What is it?" She said, "There's a guest staying at my house. Since I was born I haven't seen anyone as wealthy as he is. This man's horse doesn't eat grass or drink water like other horses. He drinks perfume, and instead of grass he eats kola nuts. Also, this boy makes a fire with incense instead of wood. Gold and silver are like sand to him." "How can I meet him?" the girl asked. "I'll return home," replied the old woman. "You make some delicious food and have a servant bring it to him." The girl agreed that this was a good way to meet him, and she sent the food.

When the food arrived the old woman got up and thanked the servant who delivered it. The old woman told the boy, "Here's some food. My granddaughter, the one I can joke with, heard that I had a guest so she sent it. She's the king's daughter, it's from their house." The boy said, "Good, thank you." He gave the servant girl who brought the food a handful of silver from his bag and filled a basket for the king's daughter. He also filled the bowl which the food was brought in with gold from his bag and said, "Take this to the king's daughter so she can buy herself something."

When the girl received the gold she decided to go and visit him. She went to the old woman's house and the boy told her, "I've come here for a reason. I heard about you in my town and God brought me here to this old woman's house. She told me all about you." He gave her his ring and they sat and chatted for a while. Then he told her, "The only reason I've come is to marry you. If it's possible let's not waste time. I'll take care of all the wedding expenses. Several days after the wedding you'll be brought to me." "Yes, I agree," she said. "I'll be brought to you, but first we must have the wedding." He told her, "Go and discuss this with your parents, and I'll go and discuss it with mine."

The boy was given a lot of money by the wealthy man who told him, "Don't hesitate to spend it all, buy everything you need." The boy paid for all of the marriage expenses and the wedding was held.

People came and spent a week celebrating. Everyone was very surprised and wondered how it was possible for a stranger to come and marry the king's daughter. The girl had everything she wanted.

The king's daughter married the boy because the old woman told her that he was wealthy. But everyone knows that greed is the key to trouble. Events unfolded quickly for the boy. After the wedding the king's daughter was brought to his home. Time passed and they lived together like this.

Then by some misfortune someone told the boy's real father the news of his son's success. He was told about the marriage and his son's wealth as well as the name of the town he lived in. The man had thought that his son was dead. But now, the man, who was still very poor, disguised himself in tattered clothes and set out for his son's town. He slept here and there along the way until God brought him to the town of the wealthy man who had adopted the boy. He asked for directions to the wealthy man's house and someone gave them to him. Some people said not to tell him, but others suggested they show him the way.

The man went to the house and greeted the wealthy man. The wealthy man was kind and did not judge people even if they were poor. They greeted each other and the wealthy man invited him in. When the poor man entered the room his son was there, but he did not recognize the boy. The wealthy man welcomed him, but the boy was unhappy.

The poor man said he had come because he heard his son was there. He said, "Someone told me that a wealthy man took my son." The poor man said that he had come to take back his son and that if he was refused he would go to a judge. The boy asked the man, "If you saw your son would you recognize him?" "Of course," said the man. The wealthy man asked him, "Where did you lose your son?" "In the bush," he answered. "Well, the boy you see here is your son," the wealthy man said. "I want you to let him stay here and keep this a secret for me. I'm a wealthy man, but I don't have a son or a grandchild. Stay here and I'll give you a house and money to buy things. Please try and understand my situation. I have one foot on earth and one foot in Paradise. When I die all of my wealth will become yours." The man said he would rather die of poverty. He repeated that he had come to take back his son and that if he didn't get him he would go to a judge. The wealthy man said, "I don't want to get into a long argument which will attract many people. I agree to return your son to you. Prepare to leave and we'll accompany you." He added, "I hope that when your son thinks of me and sees that I've helped him he comes to visit."

The boy went and told his wife that he was going to accompany the guest on part of his return journey. He did not tell her what had really happened.

They travelled until they came to the place where the man had found the blood-covered boy lying in a bit of shade. When they arrived at this place the wealthy man asked the poor man, "Do you recognize this place?" The man said he did not. The wealthy man asked, "How can you not recognize this place, look at it carefully." The poor man looked north, south, east and west. He repeated, "Look carefully." The wealthy man told him, "It was at this tree that you tried to kill your son. It was here I found him. I've already told you what I thought would be best for all of us. Look at your son."

The wealthy man drew his sword and told the boy, "Take it. Between him and me you must kill one of us. If you choose to kill me, you'll return to inherit all of my wealth. If you kill your father, we'll go and dig a grave and bury him." The boy decided to kill his father with whom he had lived in poverty; his father with whom he weeded the field for planting; his father who said that he would plant millet to buy a horse; his father who tried to kill him when he said that he would ride the horse; his father who left him in the sun until the vultures came. But because he was still alive, God led the wealthy man to the boy. Even though the poor man was offered money and a house to live in he refused. Even if the son killed the wealthy man to inherit the money, his father would kill him to get the inheritance. Therefore the boy killed his real father.

# GLOSSARY

Algaita. A reed wind instrument.

Antimony. In a finely powdered form it is applied to the edges of the eyelids and eyebrows as a cosmetic.

Aya. A small nut which is born from tiger-nut grass and eaten as a snack.

Boka. A traditional doctor.

Dimniya. A sweet plum-like fruit.

Dodo. An ogre-like creature which is feared and considered dangerous.

Fulbe. A people, a segment of whom are transhumant herders of goats, sheep and especially cattle. The men and the women braid their hair.

Fura. A combination of pounded millet, milk and sugar which is eaten out of a calabash bowl with a ladle.

Gammo. A long, thin strip of cloth which is rolled into a disk and placed on the head when carrying a load.

Goge. A stringed instrument which is played with a bow.

Jinn. A spirit.

Kilishi. Thin strips of dried, spiced meat.

Koko.     A combination of pounded millet, water, tamarind juice and sugar which is eaten like fura.

Malam.    A Koranic scholar. He is highly respected and often consulted for advice. The plural form of this word is malamai.

Muezzin.  In Islam, the person who performs the five daily calls to prayer.

Tuwo.     The staple food of the Hausa, usually pounded millet, which is eaten with a sauce.

# MONOGRAPHS IN INTERNATIONAL STUDIES

ISBN Prefix 0-89680-

**Africa Series**

38. Wright, Donald R. *Oral Traditions From the Gambia: Volume II, Family Elders.* 1980. 200pp.
084-9 $15.00

43. Harik, Elsa M. and Donald G. Schilling. *The Politics of Education in Colonial Algeria and Kenya.* 1984. 102pp.
117-9 $12.50

45. Keto, C. Tsehloane. *American-South African Relations 1784–1980: Review and Select Bibliography.* 1985. 159pp.
128-4 $11.00

46. Burness, Don, and Mary-Lou Burness, eds. *Wanasema: Conversations with African Writers.* 1985. 95pp.
129-2 $11.00

47. Switzer, Les. *Media and Dependency in South Africa: A Case Study of the Press and the Ciskei "Homeland."* 1985. 80pp.
130-6 $10.00

48. Heggoy, Alf Andrew. *The French Conquest of Algiers, 1830: An Algerian Oral Tradition.* 1986. 101pp.
131-4 $11.00

49. Hart, Ursula Kingsmill. *Two Ladies of Colonial Algeria: The Lives and Times of Aurelie Picard and Isabelle Eberhardt.* 1987. 156pp.
143-8 $11.00

51. Clayton, Anthony, and David Killingray. *Khaki and Blue: Military and Police in British Colonial Africa.* 1989. 235pp.
147-0 $18.00

52. Northrup, David. *Beyond the Bend in the River: African Labor in Eastern Zaire, 1864-1940.* 1988. 195pp.
151-9 $15.00

53. Makinde, M. Akin. *African Philosophy, Culture, and Traditional Medicine.* 1988. 175pp.
152-7                $13.00

54. Parson, Jack ed. *Succession to High Office in Botswana. Three Case Studies.* 1990. 443pp.
157-8                $20.00

55. Burness, Don. *A Horse of White Clouds.* 1989. 193pp.
158-6                $12.00

56. Staudinger, Paul. *In the Heart of the Hausa States.* Tr. by Johanna Moody. 1990. 2 vols. 653pp.
160-8                $35.00

57. Sikainga, Ahmad Alawad. *The Western Bahr Al-Ghazal Under British Rule: 1898-1956.* 1991. 183pp.
161-6                $15.00

58. Wilson, Louis E. *The Krobo People of Ghana to 1892: A Political and Social History.* 1991. 254pp.
164-0                $20.00

59. du Toit, Brian M. *Cannabis, Alcohol, and the South African Student: Adolescent Drug Use 1974-1985.* 1991. 166pp.
166-7                $17.00

60. Falola, Toyin, ed. *The Political Economy of Health in Africa.* 1992. 254pp.
168-3                $17.00

61. Kiros, Tedros. *Moral Philosophy and Development: The Human Condition in Africa.* 1992. 178pp.
171-3                $18.00

62. Burness, Don. *Echoes of the Sunbird: An Anthology of Contemporary African Poetry.* 1993. 198pp.
173-X                $17.00

63. Glew, Robert S., and Chaibou Babalé. *Hausa Folktales from Niger.* 1993. 136pp.
176-4                $15.00

## Latin America Series

9.  Tata, Robert J. *Structural Changes in Puerto Rico's Economy: 1947-1976.* 1981. xiv, 104pp.
    107-1                                                        $11.00

11. O'Shaughnessy, Laura N., and Louis H. Serra. *Church and Revolution in Nicaragua.* 1986. 118pp.
    126-8                                                        $11.00

12. Wallace, Brian. *Ownership and Development: A comparison of Domestic and Foreign Investment in Colombian Manufacturing.* 1987. 186pp.
    145-4                                                        $10.00

13. Henderson, James D. *Conservative Thought in Latin America: The Ideas of Laureano Gomez.* 1988. 150pp.
    148-9                                                        $13.00

14. Summ, G. Harvey, and Tom Kelly. *The Good Neighbors: America, Panama, and the 1977 Canal Treaties.* 1988. 135pp.
    149-7                                                        $13.00

15. Peritore, Patrick. *Socialism, Communism, and Liberation Theology in Brazil: An Opinion Survey Using Q-Methodology.* 1990. 245pp.
    156-X                                                        $15.00

16. Alexander, Robert J. *Juscelino Kubitschek and the Development of Brazil.* 1991. 429pp.
    163-2                                                        $25.00

17. Mijeski, Kenneth J., ed. *The Nicaraguan Constitution of 1987: English Translation and Commentary.* 1990. 355pp.
    165-9                                                        $25.00

18. Finnegan, Pamela May. *The Tension of Paradox: José Donoso's The Obscene Bird of Night as Spiritual Exercises.* 1992. 179pp.
    169-1                                                        $15.00

19. Sung Ho Kim and Thomas W. Walker, eds., *Perspectives on War and Peace in Central America*. 1992. 150pp.
172-1          $14.00

## Southeast Asia Series

47. Wessing, Robert. *Cosmology and Social Behavior in a West Javanese Settlement*. 1978. 200pp.
072-5          $12.00

56A. Duiker, William J. *Vietnam Since the Fall of Saigon*. Updated edition. 1989. 383pp.
162-4          $17.00

64. Dardjowidjojo, Soenjono. *Vocabulary Building in Indonesian: An Advanced Reader*. 1984. xviii, 256pp.
118-7          $26.00

65. Errington, J. Joseph. *Language and Social Change in Java: Linguistic Reflexes of Modernization in a Traditional Royal Polity*. 1985. xiv, 211pp.
120-9          $20.00

66. Binh, Tran Tu. *The Red Earth: A Vietnamese Memoir of Life on a Colonial Rubber Plantation*. Tr. by John Spragens. Ed. by David Marr. 1985. xii, 98pp.
119-5          $11.00

68. Syukri, Ibrahim. *History of the Malay Kingdom of Patani*. Tr. by Connor Bailey and John N. Miksic. 1985. xix, 113pp.
123-3          $12.00

69. Keeler, Ward. *Javanese: A Cultural Approach*. 1984. xxxvi, 522pp., Third printing 1992.
121-7          $25.00

70. Wilson, Constance M., and Lucien M. Hanks. *Burma-Thailand Frontier Over Sixteen Decades: Three Descriptive Documents*. 1985. x, 128pp.
124-1          $11.00

71. Thomas, Lynn L., and Franz von Benda-Beckmann, eds. *Change and Continuity in Minangkabau: Local, Regional, and Historical Perspectives on West Sumatra.* 1986. 363pp.
127-6                                                            $16.00

72. Reid, Anthony, and Oki Akira, eds. *The Japanese Experience in Indonesia: Selected Memoirs of 1942-1945.* 1986. 411pp., 20 illus.
132-2                                                            $20.00

73. Smirenskaia, Zhanna D. *Peasants in Asia: Social Consciousness and Social Struggle.* Tr. by Michael J. Buckley. 1987. 248pp.
134-9                                                            $14.00

74. McArthur, M.S.H. *Report on Brunei in 1904.* Ed. by A.V.M. Horton. 1987. 304pp.
135-7                                                            $15.00

75. Lockard, Craig Alan. *From Kampung to City. A Social History of Kuching Malaysia 1820-1970.* 1987. 311pp.
136-5                                                            $16.00

76. McGinn, Richard. *Studies in Austronesian Linguistics.* 1988. 492pp.
137-3                                                            $20.00

77. Muego, Benjamin N. *Spectator Society: The Philippines Under Martial Rule.* 1988. 232pp.
138-1                                                            $15.00

79. Walton, Susan Pratt. *Mode in Javanese Music.* 1987. 279pp.
144-6                                                            $15.00

80. Nguyen Anh Tuan. *South Vietnam Trial and Experience: A Challenge for Development.* 1987. 482pp.
141-1                                                            $18.00

81. Van der Veur, Paul W., ed. *Toward a Glorious Indonesia: Reminiscences and Observations of Dr. Soetomo.* 1987. 367pp.
142-X                                                            $16.00

82. Spores, John C. *Running Amok: An Historical Inquiry.* 1988. 190pp.
140-3          $13.00

83. Malaka. *From Jail to Jail.* Tr. and ed. by Helen Jarvis. 1990. 3 vols. 1,226pp.
150-0          $55.00

84. Devas, Nick. *Financing Local Government in Indonesia.* 1989. 344pp.
153-5          $16.00

85. Suryadinata, Leo. *Military Ascendancy and Political Culture: A Study of Indonesia's Golkar.* 1989. 250pp.
154-3          $18.00

86. Williams, Michael. *Communism, Religion, and Revolt in Banten.* 1990. 356pp.
155-1          $14.00

87. Hudak, Thomas John. *The Indigenization of Pali Meters in Thai Poetry.* 1990. 237pp.
159-4          $15.00

88. Lay, Ma Ma. *Not Out of Hate: A Novel of Burma.* Tr. by Margaret Aung-Thwin. Ed. by William Frederick. 1991. 222pp.
167-5          $20.00

89. Anwar, Chairil. *The Voice of the Night: Complete Poetry and Prose of Anwar Chairil.* 1993. Revised Edition. Tr. by Burton Raffel. 180pp.

         $17.00

90. Hudak, Thomas John, tr. *The Tale of Prince Samuttakote: A Buddhist Epic from Thailand.* 1993. 275pp.
174-8          $20.00

91. Roskies, D. M., ed. *Text/Politics in Island Southeast Asia: Essays in Interpretation.* 1993. 321pp.
175-6          $25.00

## ORDERING INFORMATION

Orders for titles in the Monographs in International Studies series may be placed through the Ohio University Press, Scott Quadrangle, Athens, Ohio 45701-2979 or through any local bookstore. Individuals should remit payment by check, VISA, or MasterCard.* People ordering from the United Kingdom, Continental Europe, the Middle East, and Africa should order through Academic and University Publishers Group, 1 Gower Street, London WC1E, England. Orders from the Pacific Region, Asia, Australia, and New Zealand should be sent to East-West Export Books, c/o the University of Hawaii Press, 2840 Kolowalu Street, Honolulu, Hawaii 96822, USA.

Other individuals ordering from outside of the U.S. should remit in U.S. funds to Ohio University Press either by International Money Order or by a check drawn on a U.S. bank.** Most out-of-print titles may be ordered from University Microfilms, Inc., 300 North Zeeb Road, Ann Arbor, Michigan 48106, USA.

Prices are subject to change without notice.

---

\* Please include $3.00 for the first book and 75¢ for each additional book for shipping and handling.

\** Please include $4.00 for the first book and 75¢ for each additional book for foreign shipping and handling.